Young Onset Dementia

of related interest

Intellectual Disability and Dementia
Research into Practice
Edited by Karen Watchman
ISBN 978 1 84905 422 5
eISBN 978 0 85700 796 4

Living Better with Dementia
Good Practice and Innovation for the Future
Shibley Rahman
Forewords by Kate Swaffer, Chris Roberts and Beth Britton
ISBN 978 1 84905 600 7
eISBN 978 1 78450 062 7

What the hell happened to my brain?
Living Beyond Dementia
Kate Swaffer
ISBN 978 1 84905 608 3
eISBN 978 1 78450 073 3

Who will I be when I die?
Christine Bryden
ISBN 978 1 84905 312 9
eISBN 978 0 85700 645 5

Losing Clive to Younger Onset Dementia
One Family's Story
Helen Beaumont
ISBN 978 1 84310 480 3
eISBN 978 1 84642 862 3

Young Onset
Dementia

A Guide to Recognition, Diagnosis,
and Supporting Individuals with
Dementia and Their Families

HILDA HAYO, ALISON WARD,
and JACQUELINE PARKES

Foreword by WENDY MITCHELL

Jessica Kingsley *Publishers*
London and Philadelphia

First published in 2018
by Jessica Kingsley Publishers
73 Collier Street
London N1 9BE, UK
and
400 Market Street, Suite 400
Philadelphia, PA 19106, USA

www.jkp.com

Library of Congress Cataloging in Publication Data
Names: Hayo, Hilda, author. | Ward, Alison, 1973- author. | Parkes,
   Jacqueline, author.
Title: Young onset dementia : a guide to recognition, diagnosis, and
   supporting individuals with dementia and their families / Hilda Hayo,
   Alison Ward, and Jacqueline Parkes.
Description: London ; Philadelphia : Jessica Kingsley Publishers, 2018. |
   Includes bibliographical references and index.
Identifiers: LCCN 2017045592 | ISBN 9781785921179 (alk. paper)
Subjects: | MESH: Dementia--diagnosis | Dementia--therapy | Social Work | Age
   of Onset | Social Support | Early Diagnosis | Middle Aged | United Kingdom
   | Case Reports
Classification: LCC RC521 | NLM WM 220 | DDC 616.8/31075-
   -dc23 LC record available at https://lccn.loc.gov/2017045592

British Library Cataloguing in Publication Data
A CIP catalogue record for this book is available from the British Library

ISBN 978 1 78592 117 9
eISBN 978 1 78450 383 3

Printed and bound in Great Britain

Acknowledgements

The authors would like to thank all those who contributed to this book. Giving voice to personal experiences can be an incredibly challenging thing to do but it is important that these voices are heard. The personal experiences of those who are living with young onset dementia and who are caring for a person with young onset dementia need to be heard by the health and social care professions, because these real and often difficult journeys provide greater understanding of what it means to live with young onset dementia and thus greater learning about how we can support the individual with the dementia, as well as the friends and family around them. This book would not have been possible without the time, generosity and honesty of the families and people with dementia who spoke with the authors about their journeys. These were sometimes hard to tell, sometimes funny and sometimes cathartic. Together we aim to raise greater awareness of young onset dementia and to encourage greater support for everyone living with this condition.

Contents

Foreword

Those diagnosed with young onset dementia rarely fit the stereotypical image of someone with dementia. As someone who has gone through a process of diagnosis, abandonment, and being met by a lack of understanding from healthcare practitioners, it is refreshing to read a book dedicated to the unique challenges faced by those of working age. If dealt with appropriately and offered the right support needed by each individual, it can turn what is often a devastating diagnosis into something less fearful. Health and social care practitioners with the right knowledge and a positive outlook on support can give hope rather than despair, encouragement rather than finality. This book can give them that knowledge and understanding. It deals with the circumstances currently so often forgotten – the effect on family relationships, loneliness and meaningful continuation of employment and activities.

People with dementia are always emphasising that when we get a diagnosis, so too do our family and friends. They too need support and education and I was pleased to read how 'family-centred care' is truly at the heart of this book.

For those health and social care practitioners reading this book, it can give them knowledge and insight needed to deliver a richer and more positive message to people going through diagnosis and post-diagnosis. Dementia is a bummer of a diagnosis to get at any age, but for those diagnosed with young onset, with life plans still ahead of them, it can appear a bigger tragedy. Yet, if dealt with correctly by those at the very heart of our care, it can remove the feeling of 'the end' and instead promote the beginning of a different life, certainly, but one of adapting and hopefully facing with less fear.

This book is essential reading for any health and social care practitioners involved in or interested in understanding the practical and emotional support needed by those with young onset dementia. Thank you to the authors for providing this much-needed resource.

Please feel free to read my blog on living with dementia: www.whichmeamitoday.wordpress.com, or follow me on Twitter: @WendyPMitchell.

Wendy Mitchell, author, blogger, and living with dementia
September 2017

Introduction

Receiving a formal diagnosis of dementia can be devastating at any age, but for people who are of working age it can have significant life-changing consequences for them and their families. As the person with dementia experiences progressive cognitive changes, they may decide to give up work. Their main family carer may need to work more flexibly, reduce their hours, or leave employment altogether to care for them. Family finances may come under pressure, preventing the family members being able to engage as actively as they once did in hobbies, interests, or social activities. Families, as well as the person with the diagnosis, can begin to feel socially isolated and lonely as it becomes increasingly more challenging to maintain an active and meaningful social life outside of the family home. The younger person with a diagnosis may feel increasingly frustrated as they feel their independence is being gradually eroded and they no longer feel they have a purpose in life. Faced with the behavioural, personality, and memory changes that their loved one is experiencing, family members may also experience a plethora of emotions. These may vary between being protective and wanting to keep them safe, through to embarrassment at their unpredictable behaviour in public, and resentment and guilt at seeing their relationship change and their future life plans together fade away.

For health and social care practitioners who work with young people with dementia, it is essential that they listen to the 'life stories' of all involved in the journey, getting to know their likes, dislikes, interests, hobbies, knowledge, skills, existing mental capacities and capabilities, personal circumstances, fears, hopes, and aspirations. Planning the future together with the family will help them to learn to adapt and cope better with the diagnosis and ensure that they stay as independent, socially connected, and supported for as long as possible together at home. This book is designed for all health and social practitioners who work on a daily basis with people with young onset dementia and their families. It provides a greater understanding of what young onset dementia is, the types of dementia, and their impact on different aspects of family and individuals' lives. This will be supported by case studies and quotes taken from people living with young onset dementia and their family to provide personal stories which exemplify the narrative of the book. These will sit alongside learning points and recommendations for service provision and how health and social care practitioners can provide best practice support. A resources section is included at the end of the book to assist with further learning and identification of service provision. Ultimately, it has been written to enhance the knowledge of those who support younger people with dementia so they can provide truly family centred care.

While dementia is considered to affect those in old age and to be a natural part of ageing, it can affect people under the age of 65 years. Conservative estimates indicate that approximately 42,000 people of working age could be living with a diagnosis of dementia in the UK; however, due to difficulties with diagnosis and reporting, this figure could be under-representative of the actual number of people living with the diagnosis (Alzheimer's Society 2014). Dementia is often categorised as late onset dementia (over 65 years of age) and young onset dementia or working age dementia (under 65 years of age) (Bakker 2013; van Vliet *et al.* 2012). People with young onset dementia are typically in their 40s–60s but rare cases have been found in young adulthood and in people aged in their 30s (Armari, Jarmolowicz and Panegyres 2013; Imrie, Jacklin and Mathieson 2008).

It is difficult to diagnose dementia in a younger person, particularly in the early stages of the disease, as the initial signs often differ from those observed in individuals with a later onset (van Vliet *et al.* 2012). There are also differences in the types of dementia diagnosed in the over and under 65 age groups (see Table i.1).

Table i.1 Most common types of dementia in the over 65 year group (Prince *et al.* 2014) and the under 65 year group (Rossor *et al.* 2010; YoungDementia UK 2017)

Type of dementia	Proportion of different types of dementia (%) in the under 65 year age group	Proportion of different types of dementia (%) in the over 65 year age group
Alzheimer's disease	34%	62%
Vascular dementia	18%	17%
Mixed dementia	Figures not included in the study.	10%
Dementia with Lewy bodies	7%	4%
Frontotemporal dementia	12%	2%
Alcohol related brain impairment	10%	Figures not included in the study.
Other	19%	5%

There are a greater number of rarer dementias (such as Huntington's Disease, Creutzfeldt-Jakob disease, alcohol related dementia and genetic forms of dementia) identified in the under 65 year age group which can lead to difficulties with finding an accurate diagnosis (Fardil *et al.* 2009, Harris and Keady 2004; McMurtray *et al.* 2006).

A number of issues feed into the difficulties, and subsequent delay, of diagnosis. People with young onset dementia may present with symptoms other than memory loss, such as behavioural and mood changes, problems with speech or decision making (Armari *et al.* 2013; Koedam *et al.* 2010), more atypical presentations than might be expected. As a result, the presentation of dementia can be misdiagnosed for depression, stress, menopause, or other illnesses (Alzheimer's Society 2014; Armari *et al.* 2013; Bakker *et al.* 2010), or associated with changes in personal circumstances, for example the loss of employment or breakdown of a relationship. This can result in a three-to-five year delay to receiving a diagnosis of young onset dementia. Furthermore, lack of awareness of young onset dementia from the individual, family and GP may factor into a delayed diagnosis and the limited services available for the younger age group can further exacerbate the diagnosis. A number of issues are faced by younger people living with young onset dementia, these are summarised in Box i.1.

Box i.1: Particular issues faced by younger people living with dementia

- They may have a rare form of dementia (Rossor *et al.* 2010).

- They are more likely to have a difficulty receiving an accurate early diagnosis (van Vliet *et al.* 2010a).

- They are more likely to be misdiagnosed (Werner, Stein-Schvachman and Korczyn 2009).

- They may be in work at the time of diagnosis or have recently lost their job (Rose and Yu 2010).

- Younger people may have heavy financial commitments including: mortgage and/or children at university (Jefferies and Agrawal 2009).

- They may have dependent children (Beattie *et al.* 2004).

- Some have additional caring responsibility for parents (Arai *et al.* 2007).

- They are more likely to have a partner who still works (Allen, Oyebode and Allen 2009; Rose and Yu 2010).

- They are more likely to be physically fit and active (Armstrong 2003).

- They are more likely to have a dementia affecting behaviour and social functioning in the early stages (Rossor *et al.* 2010).

- Family members are more likely to report significantly higher psychological and physical morbidity (Rosness, Mjørud and Engedal 2011).

(adapted from Alzheimer's
Society 2014; Hayo 2016)

A study by Armari *et al.* (2013) found that families living with young onset dementia identified early diagnosis and prompt referral as a key area for service improvement. The lack of specialist post diagnostic support was reported as a significant issue for these families, which could result in social isolation and family distress (Lockeridge and Simpson 2012).

Stigma associated with dementia is central to this loss of social connectedness and can increase the feelings associated with loss of self-identity in the person with dementia (Clemerson, Walsh and Isaac 2014). Those with young onset dementia will predominantly still be living in the community within their own homes and as such their community circles can become smaller and their situation more isolating (Harris and Keady 2004; Lockeridge and Simpson 2012). With this brings the likelihood of stress and depression (Armari *et al.* 2013) and a loss of self-confidence and self-esteem through changing roles, for example, loss of employment, being cared for, potential changes in marital and parental relationships and loss of independence (Harris and Keady 2004; Green and Kleissen 2013; van Vliet *et al.* 2010a; Wawrzinczny *et al.* 2014), which may impact on a person's quality of life and wellbeing. Furthermore, people living with young onset dementia often have 'feelings of fear, grief and loss, frustration, loss of control, embarrassment, insecurity and isolation' (Tindall and Manthorpe 1997, p.243). Where these feelings may be heightened and differ from those with late onset dementia is in the unexpected nature of young onset dementia, which can often be more rapid in decline and significantly change the person's expected life course (Clemerson *et al.* 2014; Tindall and Manthorpe 1997). Clearly, the diagnosis of dementia can have a significant impact on the individual and family, both physically and psychologically, but it can also impact on how they interact with wider society (Bakker *et al.* 2008, Fardil *et al.* 2009; van Vliet *et al.* 2012). Allen, Oyebode and Allen (2009) describe a 'ripple effect' following a diagnosis of dementia, flowing through every aspect of young people's lives, from relationships with other family members, friends, school, to their hobbies and career choices. The government has identified the need to reduce loneliness and increase social connectedness for people living with dementia in the community in order to improve quality of life. Kane and Cook (2013) report that 33 per cent of people living with dementia have reported losing friends following disclosure of their diagnosis. A range of strategies have been launched to enhance public knowledge and attitudes towards dementia, and promote social inclusion and normalisation (Department of Health (DH) 2009; DH 2012). However, across the UK there is little understanding of the unique needs of people with young onset dementia and therefore limited availability of specialist services, making it difficult to access adequate support (Kane and Cook 2013).

Services are often aimed at an older age group and do not meet the social interests or physical capabilities of people with young onset dementia (Beattie *et al.* 2002; Jefferies and Agrawal 2009). Bakker and colleagues (2010) argue that services designed specifically for this younger age group can be beneficial and improve wellbeing for both the person with dementia and their families. An appropriate service provision for people living with young onset dementia is essential in ensuring that support, coping strategies, information and access to normal, everyday activities are available to the person with dementia and their families. This service provision needs to be delivered in a way that is different to the service provision for those with late onset dementia and which is unique for people living with young onset dementia (Bakker *et al.* 2010).

Provision of quality care for this group is not widely available in the UK, with Rayment and Kuruvilla (2015) calling it 'highly variable' (p.29). While the Alzheimer's Society (2014) suggests services are beginning to improve, and examples of good practice are evident (YoungDementia UK, YPWD Berkshire West and Forget-me-not Centre are some examples of the small number of dedicated services for people living with young onset dementia); however, these are not the norm (Miranda-Castillo *et al.* 2010). What these services offer is a balance between social activities and more formal support, for example gardening and walking clubs, social meal/dance evenings and one-to-one peer support. However, these services are not universally available across the UK (Rayment and Kuruvilla 2015) and evidence suggests that health service provision for young onset dementia is often inadequate (Armari *et al.* 2013; Beattie *et al.* 2002; Jefferies and Agrawal 2009) and does not provide the right 'fit' for the needs of those who have young onset dementia or for families and those who provide care for a person living with young onset dementia (Bakker *et al.* 2010; Bakker 2014; Gibson, Anderson and Acocks 2014). This can leave people feeling unsure where to find support or experiencing uncoordinated approaches to care (Rayment and Kuruvilla 2015). Lack of knowledge and understanding of young onset dementia can make access to appropriate services difficult (Alzheimer's Society 2014). Evidence suggests the focus of care is often on respite care, day care facilities, support groups and longer term care for those with late onset dementia (Bakker *et al.* 2010) and services can be inappropriate for a younger age group, not meeting their 'complex needs' and abilities (Alzheimer's Society 2014, p.4).

There is a need for age specific services for those with young onset dementia, because evidence suggests that people living with young onset dementia and their families want different services and do not want to access day facilities with elderly people with dementia, whose symptoms and activity levels may differ greatly (Green and Kleissen 2013; Parkes, Hayo and Sixsmith 2012). National Institute for Health and Care Excellence (NICE) dementia clinical guidelines (2006) state that persons living with young onset dementia have 'specialist requirements' and services need to be provided to meet their care, while the Alzheimer's Society (2014) recommend services are developed to 'maintain day-to-day skills, friendships, hobbies and interests', helping people to be active and remain living in their community (p.4). NICE guidelines recommend that services should encourage people with dementia to live independently, to develop skills, 'minimise the need for support' and people should have the opportunity to engage in activities which stimulate them cognitively (NICE 2006, p.25). Recent studies show that services which provide 'normalisation' for person living with young onset dementia are needed (Clemerson *et al.* 2013; Parkes *et al.* 2012; Pipon-Young *et al.* 2012) and offering a place where a person living with young onset dementia can socialise together, share experiences and undertake, good quality, 'meaningful' activities are required (Green and Kleissen 2013; Harris and Keady 2004; Roach and Drummond 2014).

Bakker and colleagues' (2010) case study of a person with young onset dementia identifies further benefits for the value of appropriate services, as it was reported that provision of adequate services and support helped to reduce behavioural issues from the person living with young onset dementia, provided respite for their family carer and improved the wellbeing of both individuals.

Recommendations for service provision for people living with dementia suggest it should be flexible (Jefferies and Agrawal 2009), meet the needs of family, carers and people living with dementia (Harris and Keady 2004; NICE 2006), be meaningful, focused on emotional as well as problem solving activities (Alzheimer's Society 2010; Harris and Keady 2004; Martin *et al.* 2012), seek to improve quality of life and wellbeing, 'promote personal dignity' (Alzheimer's Society 2010; Miranda-Castillo *et al.* 2010) and be provided within a community setting (WHO 2012). The NICE guidelines (2006) also encourage caregivers and family members to engage in activities with the person with dementia, as this inclusion of caregiver support in activities can benefit both. This is borne out in research where 'family orientated' support and information sharing can be beneficial and is something families want (Barca *et al.* 2014). Wawrziczny and colleagues (2014) also advocate for the development of services for couples with a focus on communication, particularly after early diagnosis of the dementia. Finally, Westera and colleagues (2014) identified that services which sought to address or work within the following criteria would be working to best practice: a focus on the individual; family approach; provision of social activities; incorporating formal services; and linking these with the latest legislation and policy. There is a growing evidence base through policy, research and anecdotal accounts on how to best provide services for people living with young onset dementia and what this service provision should look like to best support quality of life, wellbeing and person-centred care; however, there seems to be a gap in translating this into practice and the actual services on the ground are not yet widely or universally available across the UK.

The following case study provides an overview of many of the issues which have been raised in this Introduction and which will be developed further throughout the book. Roy and Kay's story exemplifies the complexities of living with a diagnosis of young onset dementia and identifies the ways that services can both support and hinder depending on their approach.

CASE STUDY i.1

Kay's journey to a formal diagnosis of dementia has been extremely complex and difficult for both her and her long-term partner of 17 years, Roy. Initial signs and symptoms first started to emerge when Kay was 47 years old, while she was still working as a care home manager. Prior to receiving a diagnosis, Kay's employers noticed changes in her which resulted in them deciding that it was best that she stop working. Roy explains that prior to the early signs and symptoms emerging, Kay was a bright, 'bubbly' person; however, over the last seven years, he has since seen significant changes in her personality, which has not been helped by her tendency to 'drink' heavily.

Kay has become more demonstrative, cross, judgemental, less inhibited and less patient. She shows signs of some memory loss. Her forgetfulness and distractibility can leave her feeling confused, frustrated, and angry. She feels her choices and independence are being gradually taken away from her as she no longer has her car, and it has become *'too dangerous for her to cook unsupported as she can often leave the oven or gas on'. She* also finds it difficult to *'follow television programmes'*. Having no concept of the date or time, Kay can go missing for hours. Roy has had some very difficult and stressful times searching their local town and neighbourhood to find Kay, which on occasions has led to police involvement. They have found Kay wondering the streets. *'Being a very private person'*, Roy has found himself having to *'pour his life and heart out'* telling different services his story each time, which can be very distressing. Roy says that he never stops worrying when Kay goes out on her own. He understands that she needs to have this freedom but finds it difficult as he never knows when or if she will return home. He has learnt to accept the situation but he explains that he will never stop worrying.

Kay has 'good and bad days' and she is better in the morning than the afternoon or evenings. With support, she can still enjoy cooking, *'being able to make a good loaf of bread',* attend her activity and social groups, and walk into the local town on her own; however, while she still wants to be active and do lots of things, she can tire very quickly, which can exacerbate her symptoms and leave her feeling so exhausted, she can sleep for two or three days at a time. Conversely, Kay can also be quite a light sleeper, finding it difficult to get off to sleep. Her eating habits have also changed. Where once she had a savoury palate, she now prefers sweet foods, in particular chocolate.

Seven years on, and now aged 54, Kay has recently been told that she has a likely diagnosis of a frontotemporal dementia, but this still is yet to be officially confirmed. Kay has had, and continues to have, numerous scans and tests. Not knowing has been difficult for both Roy and Kay, who want to know and understand what her symptoms mean. For Kay, especially, she likes to be able to compartmentalise and label things and the uncertainty around her diagnosis has been difficult to manage. A lack of a confirmed diagnosis has also meant that they have not been able to access any care or join any support groups until very recently.

Dementia has affected both Kay and Roy; when Roy talks of how life has changed, he talks about 'we' and 'us', emphasising that dementia is not just about the individual but has affected the whole family. Where once Roy and Kay had individual aspects to their lives, they are now *'in each other's pockets 24/7'.* Both have made changes to their employment, Kay having to give up work and Roy now working predominantly from home. Roy has been fortunate with the support he receives from his employers, who have enabled him to continue to work and be flexible in his working hours. Roy explains that he often works in the early hours or late at night, while Kay is asleep, so that he has time to dedicate to his work. During the day Roy's time is often taken up with providing care for Kay. However, on occasions he still needs to travel for work, which can cause great stress. With good respite now available to Roy, this stress has been minimised but he still tries to limit his time away from Kay. Roy also describes how their lives have become increasingly isolated. There are a number of reasons for this, including a house-move to a new area to live in a house which is better suited to Kay's needs, the loss of Kay's driving license, and also that they have made a conscious decision to withdraw. This withdrawal stems from the stigma associated with dementia both from themselves and others, feelings of not wanting to deal with any potentially embarrassing behaviour and people's lack of understanding of dementia. Their plans for a future retirement in Tenerife have been put on hold, although they are still enjoying holidays to their favourite village in Tenerife, where Kay feels at home and safe. However, travel is becoming increasingly more difficult for Kay. She finds the crowds at airports overwhelming and they now require special assistance to navigate the airport. They recently moved to a bungalow so that Kay is near a small town centre which she can easily walk to. This is seen as a final house move as Kay currently has a good care manager who is knowledgeable of the system and care provision in their locality, and to move again would result in the loss of this care package, as it is not easy to transfer care from one area to another.

Kay is regularly seen by a social worker and a neuro-physiologist; however, they generally see her at the same time of day on the same day of the week for these appointments. While this consistency can be supportive for a person with dementia, Roy explains that Kay is able to 'perform' better on tests as a result, as she knows the day of the week her visits occur and can prepare for these. The visits also take place in the morning, when Kay tends to feel better. To these professionals, Kay's condition is not considered to be having a big impact on her life, but Roy is keen to stress that they see Kay on her good days, when she has prepared for the visits. They do not see the days when Kay is tired, agitated and finding her dementia difficult to manage or, as Roy describes it, *'falling off the cliff'*. Furthermore, Roy has never been asked for his input in any of the assessments with Kay. When Kay sees her support worker, she often can't remember what they have discussed and cannot keep Roy informed of their decisions. Roy has been excluded from these meetings, sometimes on the request of Kay. He has never been asked how he, as a carer, is managing or asked what support he needs. Roy states that he sees the good and the bad days, but feels let down by health and social care professionals as he has no say in the care and treatment Kay receives. This has even led to the social worker deciding that Kay should live in her own independent accommodation, without consultation with Roy. Roy feels that as he and Kay are not married his opinion is disregarded. Roy feels very strongly that health and social care professionals should know both sides of the story and not defer solely to the person with dementia. Roy suggests that Kay should be seen at different times of the day, on different days of the week and different places to see how she responds and manages her dementia. This could provide a more rounded picture of Kay's dementia.

Roy and Kay have recently started attending a group for people with dementia and carers and this has been a source of great support for both. Kay is able to access activities which she enjoys, such as walking, and Roy is able to share his experiences with other carers who hold no judgments. Roy explains that speaking with other people who know and experience similar issues has been vital, and that it is *'good to talk to other people and know you are not on your own'*.

The book is divided into seven chapters. The Introduction has outlined the case for more specialist support, care, and interventions for this vulnerable group. Chapters 1 to 7, which are summarised below, provide health and social care practitioners and services with key information about signs and symptoms, prevention and health promotion, diagnostic processes, and post diagnostic support for people with young onset dementia and their families.

Chapter 1: Promotion of health and prevention of ill health

Recent studies provide a positive message about how individual changes in behaviour and lifestyle could prevent or delay the onset of dementia in later life. It is recommended that these changes need to be implemented in the 30–40 year age group in order to delay or reduce the incidence of dementia onset at a later stage. This chapter considers the health and lifestyle factors which could be modified in order to potentially prevent or delaying the onset of dementia, such as smoking, hypertension, obesity, and physical activity. In addition, this chapter considers the promotion of health and the prevention of physical and mental ill health of families living with young onset dementia.

Chapter 2: Groups at increased risk of young onset dementia

Two groups of people have a higher risk of young onset dementia than the general population. These are people who have intellectual disabilities, in particular Down syndrome, and those from families in which there is a genetic type of dementia. Despite the knowledge that these two groups of people have a higher risk of dementia, often the early signs are missed and an accurate diagnosis can be delayed, leading to increased distress for the person with dementia and their families. This chapter explores how dementia can be recognised at an earlier stage in people with an increased risk of young onset dementia, leading to an accurate diagnosis and timely interventions.

Chapter 3: Why early recognition and diagnosis matter

Families living with the effects of young onset dementia state that there is a lack of recognition by health and social care services that people under the age of 65 can develop a dementia. As a result there is a substantial delay in referral and diagnosis that can lead to significant family distress and relationship difficulties. Once the diagnosis is given, families identify there is a lack of specialist advice and support offered which further compounds their feelings of distress and isolation. This chapter explores the epidemiology of young onset dementia, assessment and diagnosis and support for younger people living with dementia. It also identifies the need for specialist services and the nurse's role in supporting families living with the effects of young onset dementia.

Chapter 4: Post diagnostic support and intervention

This chapter will consider the interventions, services and supports that are available for people with young onset dementia and their families. It will also explore how service provision can be tailored for this group. An international and national context will be reviewed here to provide examples of best practice and to show innovative ways to provide support, such as online and peer-to-peer.

Chapter 5: The impact of young onset dementia on family relationships

This chapter will explore the impact of a diagnosis of young onset dementia on the family, exploring the spousal and parent–child relationships, and the relationships with the wider family. Understanding how to support the family as well as the person with dementia is important for health and social care professionals and therefore learning points will examine ways to support families, to support communication and understanding of the diagnosis and consider what information families need to plan and prepare for living with a diagnosis.

Chapter 6: Lonely in a social world: Maintaining social connections in young onset dementia

This chapter explores how being diagnosed with young onset dementia can impact on the maintenance of relationships and sustaining social connections. Specialist social support groups can be beneficial in reducing the effects of social isolation and loneliness in people with a diagnosis and their families. Health and social care practitioners can support both the person with dementia and their family members to retain their social connectivity and maintain their psychosocial wellbeing by accessing appropriate community-based support groups. The benefits of attending such groups include peer support, age appropriate information, and a safe and comfortable environment.

Chapter 7: Meaningful occupation and activities

The aim of this chapter is to explore how a person with dementia and/or their family carer can be supported in continued employment after receiving a diagnosis. It considers how employers can make reasonable adjustments to support their employee in continued employment. Should the individual feel no longer able to cope in paid employment, the chapter highlights how practitioners can support them to make the decision to stop working, and explore alternative meaningful occupations which will provide a sense of purpose, value, and meaning.

Conclusion

The concluding chapter reinforces the messages which are provided by the authors that younger people with a diagnosis can remain independent, socially connected, actively engaged in meaningful occupations, and at home for longer if they and their families are supported by informed and knowledgeable family-focused professional carers.

References

Allen, J., Oyebode, J.R. and Allen, J. (2009) 'Having a father with young onset dementia: The impact on wellbeing of young people.' *Dementia* 8, 4, 455–480.

Alzheimer's Society (2014) *What is young onset dementia? Factsheet 440*. London: Alzheimer's Society. Accessed on 28/08/17 at www.alzheimers.org. uk/download/downloads/id/1766/factsheet_what_is_young-onset_ dementia.pdf

Arai, A., Matsumoto, T., Ikeda, M. and Arai, Y. (2007) 'Do family caregivers perceive more difficulty when they look after patients with early onset dementia compared to those with late onset dementia?' *International Journal of Geriatric Psychiatry 22*, 12, 1255–1261.

Armari, E., Jarmolowicz, A. and Panegyres, P.K. (2013) 'The needs of patients with early onset dementia.' *American Journal of Alzheimer's Disease and Other Dementias 28*, 1, 42–46.

Armstrong, M. (2003) 'The needs of people with young onset dementia and their carers.' *Professional Nurse 18*, 12, 681–684.

Bakker, A.B., Schaufeli, W.B., Leiter, M.P. and Taris, T.W. (2008) 'Work engagement: An emerging concept in occupational health psychology.' *Work and Stress 22*, 3, 187–200.

Bakker, C., de Vugt, M.E., Vernooij-Dassen, M., van Vliet, D., Verhey, F.R.J. and Koopmans, R.T. (2010) 'Needs in early onset dementia: A qualitative case from the NeedYD study.' *American Journal of Alzheimer's Disease and Other Dementias 25*, 8, 634–640.

Bakker, C. (2013) *Young Onset Dementia: Care Needs and Service Provision.* Nijmegen: Radboud Universiteit Nijmegen.

Bakker, C. (2014) *Younger people with dementia: attuning care to fit their needs.* Conference presentation at YoungDementia UK, Oxford: *A life worth living: Young onset dementia services and support.*

Barca, M.L., Thorsen, K., Engedal, K., Haugen, P.K. and Johannessen, A. (2014) 'Nobody asked me how I felt: experiences of adult children of persons with young-onset dementia.' *International Psychogeriatrics 26*, 12, 1935–1944.

Beattie, A.M., Daker-White, G., Gilliard, J. and Means, R. (2002) 'Younger people with dementia care: a review of service needs, service provision and models of good practice.' *Ageing and Mental Health 6*, 3, 205–212.

Clemerson, G., Walsh, S. and Isaac, C. (2014) 'Towards living well with young onset dementia: An exploration of coping from the perspective of those diagnosed.' *Dementia 13*, 4, 451–466.

Department of Health (2009) Living well with dementia: A national dementia strategy. London: DH.

Department of Health (2012) Prime Minister's Challenge on Dementia: Delivering major improvements in dementia care and research by 2015. London: DH.

Fadil, H., Borazanci, A., Ait Ben Haddou, E., Yahyaoui, M., Korniychuk, E., Jaffe, S. L. and Minagar, A. (2009) 'Chapter 13 Early Onset Dementia.' *International Review of Neurobiology 84*, 245–262.

Gibson, A.K., Anderson, K.A. and Acocks, S. (2014) Exploring the service and support needs of families with early-onset Alzheimer's disease. *American Journal of Alzheimer's Disease and Other Dementias 29*, 7, 596–600.

Green, T. and Kleissen, T. (2013) 'Early onset dementia: A narrative review of the literature.' *Indian Journal of Gerontology 27*, 1, 1–18.

Harris, P. and Keady, J. (2004) 'Living with early onset dementia: Exploring the experience and developing evidence-based guidelines for practice.' *Alzheimer's Care Quarterly 5*, 2, 111–122.

Hayo, H. (2016) 'How and why does social connectedness change in families living with the effects of behavioural variant frontotemporal dementia?' Doctor of Professional Practice. Northampton: University of Northampton.

Imrie, J., Jacklin, E. and Mathieson, T. (2008) *Dementia in children, teenagers and young adults. A guide for parents, teachers and care professionals.* Stirling: The Dementia Services Development Centre, University of Stirling.

Jefferies, K. and Agrawal, N. (2009) 'Early-onset dementia.' *Advances in Psychiatric Treatment 15*, 380–388.

Kane, M. and Cook, L. (2013) *Dementia 2013: The Hidden Voice of Loneliness.* London: Alzheimer's Society.

Koedam, E.L., Lauffer, V., van der Vlies, A.E., van der Flier, W.M., Scheltens, P. and Pijnenburg, Y.A. (2010) 'Early-versus late-onset Alzheimer's disease: more than age alone.' *Journal of Alzheimer's Disease 19*, 4, 1401–1408.

Lockeridge, S. and Simpson, J. (2012) 'The experience of caring for a partner with young onset dementia: How younger carers cope.' *Dementia 12*, 633–649.

Martin, F., Turner, A., Wallace, L. M., Choudhry, K. and Bradbury, N. (2012) 'Perceived barriers to self-management for people with dementia in the early stages.' *Dementia 12*, 4, 481–493.

McMurtray, A., Clark, D.G., Christine, D. and Mendez, M.F. (2006) 'Early-onset dementia: Frequency and causes compared to late-onset dementia.' *Dementia and Geriatric Cognitive Disorders 21*, 2, 59–64.

Miranda-Castillo, C., Woods, B., Galboda, K., Oomman, S., Olojugba, C. and Orrell, M. (2010) 'Unmet needs, quality of life and support networks of people with dementia living at home.' *Health and Quality of Life Outcomes 8*, 132–146.

National Institute for Health and Care Excellence (NICE) (2006) *Dementia: Supporting people with dementia and their carers in health and social care. NICE Clinical Guideline 42.* London: NICE.

Parkes, J., Hayo, H. and Sixsmith, J. (2012) *The effects of Early Onset dementia: Developing supportive care strategies for both the sufferer and their carers.* Vienna: Alzheimer's Europe Conference October 2012.

Pipon-Young, F.E., Lee, K.M., Jones, F. and Guss, R. (2012) 'I'm not all gone, I can still speak: The experiences of younger people with dementia. An action research study.' *Dementia 11*, 5, 597–616.

Prince, M., Knapp, M., Guerchet, M., McCrone, P. *et al.* (2014) *Dementia UK: Second edition.* London: Alzheimer's Society.

Rayment, D. and Kuruvilla, T. (2015) 'Service provision for young-onset dementia in the UK.' *Progress in Neurology and Psychiatry July/August,* 28–30.

Roach, P. and Drummond, N. (2014) '"It's nice to have something to do": Early-onset dementia and maintaining purposeful activity.' *Journal of Psychiatric and Mental Health Nursing 21,* 889–895.

Rose, K. and Yu, F. (2010) 'Care considerations for persons with early onset dementia: A case studies analysis.' *Alzheimer's Care Today 11,* 3, 151–161.

Rosness, T.A., Mjørud, M. and Engedal, K. (2011) 'Quality of life and depression in carers of patients with early onset dementia.' *Ageing and Mental Health 15,* 3, 299–306.

Rossor, M.N., Fox, N.C., Mummery, C.J., Schott, J.M. and Warren, J.D. (2010) 'The diagnosis of young-onset dementia.' *The Lancet Neurology 9,* 8, 793–806.

Tindall, L. and Manthorpe, J. (1997) 'Early onset dementia: A case of ill-timing?' *Journal of Mental Health 6,* 3, 237–249.

van Vliet, D., Bakker, C., Koopmans, R., Vernooij-Dassen, M., Verhey, F. and de Vugt, M. D. (2010a) 'Research protocol for the NeedYD-study (Needs in Young onset Dementia): A prospective cohort study on the needs and course of early onset dementia.' *BMC Geriatrics 10,* 1, 13–21.

van Vliet, D., de Vugt, M.D., Bakker, C., Koopmans, R. and Verhey, F. (2010b) 'Impact of early onset dementia on caregivers: A review.' *International Journal of Geriatric Psychiatry 25,* 1091–1100.

van Vliet, D., De Vugt, M.E., Aalten, P., Bakker, C. *et al.* (2012) 'Prevalence of neuropsychiatric symptoms in young-onset compared to late-onset Alzheimer's disease – part 1: Findings of the two-year longitudinal NeedYD-study.' *Dementia and Geriatric Cognitive Disorders 34,* 5–6, 319–327.

Wawrziczny, E., Antoine, P., Ducharme, F., Kergoat, M-J. and Pasquier, F. (2016) 'Couples' experiences with early-onset dementia: An interpretative phenomenological analysis of dyadic dynamics.' *Dementia 15,* 5, 1082–1099.

Werner, P., Stein-Shvachman, I. and Korczyn, A.D. (2009) 'Early onset dementia: clinical and social aspects.' *International Psychogeriatrics 21,* 4, 631–636.

Westera, A., Fildes, D., Duncan, C., Samsa, P., Capell, J., Grootemaat, P. and Sansoni, J. (2014) *Final Report: Literature Review and Needs and Feasibility Assessment of Services for People with Younger Onset Dementia.* Centre for Health Service Development, University of Wollongong: Australia.

World Health Organisation (WHO) (2012) *Dementia: A public health priority.* UK: EHO Library Cataloguing.

YoungDementia UK (2017) *Young onset dementia facts and figures.* Oxford: YDUK. Accessed 20/08/17 at www.youngdementiauk.org/young-onset-dementia-facts-figures

Promotion of Health and Prevention of Ill Health in Reducing Incidence of Dementia

Rationale

Recent studies provide a positive message about the way individual changes in behaviour and lifestyle could reduce the incidence or delay the onset of some dementias in later life, particularly Alzheimer's disease and vascular dementia. In 2014, key UK health and dementia representatives met to discuss the need for greater information and strategic policy around recognition of the risks for dementia or cognitive decline, especially those which are modifiable and may lead to reduced incidence of dementia or delay the onset of dementia. The Blackfriars Consensus (Lincoln *et al.* 2014) recognised the main modifiable risk factors as: smoking, poor diet, physical inactivity, alcohol consumption, and brain injury, with additional associations to hypertension, cardiovascular disease, obesity and diabetes. Furthermore, it was acknowledged there is a need for improved health promotion to encourage health throughout a person's life, their workplace and through increased social engagement.

The importance of promoting health factors which could reduce the incidence of dementia in the population is associated with the rising cost of dementia; current figures estimate that dementia costs more than heart disease, stroke or cancer, at £26.3 billion a year in the UK (Public Health England 2016). Long term, an investment in health promotion could not only save the health and social sectors money, but may also result in people living a healthier and more fulfilling life into old age.

Learning objectives

The learning objectives for this chapter are to:

- Identify the modifiable and non-modifiable risks factors associated with dementia.

- Consider ways to promote a healthier lifestyle.

- Identify the value of early interventions.

- Identify ways in which the person living with a dementia and their carer/families can benefit from improved health and lifestyle choices.

Introduction

Much research has gone into finding a cure for dementia, however, currently no cure has been found. What has become a more recent focus for research and policy is understanding the risk and preventative factors of dementia and whether it is possible to delay or reduce the incidence of dementia. There are a number of risk factors associated with dementia, some which are not changeable, or non-modifiable, such as a person's genetics, gender, ethnicity or age, but there are others which people can take steps to modify, such as lifestyle behaviours (Alzheimer's Society 2016a; Public Health England 2016; Richie *et al.* 2010). Prince and colleagues (2014) advocate that 'what is good for the heart is good for the brain', therefore exercise, diet and wellbeing are crucial factors not only for a healthy lifestyle, but also for reduced risk of developing dementia. What is also evident is that a person can change their behaviours at any time and this could still have a positive impact on a person's health and risks, as Prince and colleagues state, 'it's never too late to make these changes' (p.5). However, the Alzheimer's Society (2016a) suggests that a number of the main risk factors occur in midlife, when changes in the brain, which can result in dementia, occur, and that making changes to lifestyle behaviours between the ages of 40–64 can have a positive effect.

While the main focus of this chapter is on the preventative measures which can be promoted to maintain a healthy lifestyle, this chapter will also consider the way a person diagnosed with dementia and their carer/family may also benefit from being healthy, fit and active.

Modifiable risk factors of dementia

The main modifiable risk factors associated with dementia are: low education attainment early in life, high blood pressure in midlife, and those who smoke or have diabetes throughout their lives (Mitchell *et al.* 2016). Furthermore, taking part in physical activity, reduced obesity and reduced alcohol consumption are also associated with reduced risk of developing dementia (Lincoln *et al.* 2014; Public Health England 2016), as represented in Table 1.1. Other health risk factors also include existing medical conditions, for example Parkinson's disease, stroke and head injury. Not only are health risks important to identify, but a person's mental health, social engagement and interests may also have an important part to play, particularly to a person's overall health and wellbeing.

Table 1.1 Protective and risk factors for dementia

Protective factors	Risk factors
Reduced alcohol consumption	Alcohol consumption
Weight loss	Obesity; High blood pressure in midlife; Diabetes
Physical exercise/activity	Physical inactivity
Stop smoking	Smoking
Social activity; Hobbies/work	Depression
Cognitive activity	Educational attainment; cognitive inactivity

The life course approach considers the whole life course, whereby early development and experiences can develop resilience to later life illnesses. In the case of dementia, education, social and physical activities, and a healthy diet may impact on a person's risks of developing dementia in later life. Barnett, Hachinski and Blackwell (2013) suggest that even pre- and neonatal development can have a possible impact on the development of conditions later in life, such as on cardiovascular disease. However, early life experiences do not define our future health and midlife and later-life experiences will also have an impact (Prince *et al.* 2014), hence the importance of making positive changes at any age.

Why is there a focus on risk and preventative factors? Recent evidence suggests there may be a way for people to reduce their risks of developing dementia. A study by Norton *et al.* (2014) reported that a third of cases of Alzheimer's disease could be associated with modifiable risk factors, while Barnett *et al.* (2013) suggested that half of the risks associated with Alzheimer's disease are modifiable lifestyle risks. Furthermore, the National Institute for Health and Care Excellence (NICE 2015) suggests that vascular disease could be preventable through changes in modifiable risk factors. However, NICE recognises that other types of dementia are less well known and as such it is not yet known what risk factors are associated with these, particularly frontotemporal dementia or Lewy bodies. While changes to modifiable risk factors may have a positive impact on a person's health, it is not necessarily the case that dementia will be prevented, Prince *et al.* (2014) stress that while there may not be a way of preventing dementia, working to reduce the risks will be a positive way forward.

Much of the research conducted on health risks is with those aged over 65 years, so why might this be important for younger people? It is important to stress that it is never too early to promote a healthy lifestyle message and that ill health in midlife can be a key risk factor for development of dementia. What seems to be increasingly evident is that the changes which occur as a result of dementia may do so 10 or 20 years before a diagnosis, and so making changes earlier in life is important (Barnett *et al.* 2013; Gandy *et al.* 2017; Wang *et al.* 2017). By raising awareness and addressing these issues, it may be possible to reduce a person's risk and possibly reduce the incidence or delay the onset of dementia. Furthermore, for those who may be at a higher risk of developing dementia through non-modifiable risks, such as genetics, gender or ethnicity, maintaining a healthy lifestyle is even more important in potentially delaying any onset.

Work by Barnett *et al.* (2013) shows a clear representation of the ways in which a person can support their health and wellbeing in relation to dementia. This includes decisions made by parents when children are growing up, for example by not smoking. Our early life experiences can impact on our resilience and health, and some researchers are advocating for a 'life span' approach to the prevention of dementia: 'Prevention of dementia should start early in life, "at conception", and continue through the life span' (Scazufca *et al.* 2008, p.879). In this way people are more likely to adopt healthy habits and lifestyles that can mitigate the risks of not only dementia, but also other long-term illnesses such as diabetes or cardiovascular disease.

Diet and obesity

Obesity is considered as a potential risk factor for dementia; certainly it is linked to diabetes and heart disease – both risk factors for dementia. Being overweight can increase a person's blood pressure, which has been linked to a higher risk of dementia (NHS 2014). Baumgart *et al.* (2015) provide a summary of the evidence which sees a strong association between midlife obesity and an elevated risk of dementia. Similarly, hypertension in midlife has been identified as an associated risk factor for dementia (Corrada *et al.* 2017). Furthermore, those in midlife who have a large waist circumference and hips run a higher risk of dementia, with the fat in these areas having an impact on blood vessels and brain health (Srikanth 2017). This is supported by Albanese *et al*'s (2017) meta-analysis, looking at body mass index (BMI) of people in midlife, who found strong associations between a BMI over 30 and increased risks of developing dementia.

Eating a good diet can be an important preventative measure. The Mediterranean diet, based on vegetables, fruit and fish, is thought to be a preventative factor for Alzheimer's disease and cognitive decline (Scarmeas *et al.* 2006; Lourida *et al.* 2013), although the findings on this are not conclusive (Anstey 2017). This has been supported by longitudinal research which found eating fruit and vegetables (at least two portions a day) can be a factor in reducing the occurrence of dementia (Richie *et al.* 2010). Hogervorst (2017) also suggests that the benefits of nutrition for dementia prevention are most beneficial in midlife and before any symptoms of dementia are present, while Ritchie *et al.* (2010) advocate that the consumption of fruit and vegetables is one of the main ways to reduce the incidence of dementia, although they are less clear on how and why this might be.

Alzheimer's Research UK (2015a) advocate that people follow the 'eatwell plate' whereby a balanced diet is consumed which is low in salts, saturated fats and sugars. Eating a nutritionally balanced diet is recommended to help reduce cholesterol, reduce weight and therefore reduce the likelihood of heart disease and other associated conditions, all of which could have preventative measures for dementia.

Physical exercise

Physical activity, or lack of it, could be a risk factor associated with the onset of dementia. This may be particularly true for those who have reduced physical activity in mid to later adult life. Studies have suggested that the effects of some form of physical exercise could reduce the risk of the onset of dementia (Hooghiemstra *et al.* 2012) and that it can have a positive impact on cognitive function for those with dementia (Groot *et al.* 2016). Exercise has been linked with lower mortality rates for heart disease and diabetes, reduced risk of high blood pressure and other medical problems associated with dementia (Yaffe *et al.* 2003; Prince *et al.* 2014; Alzheimer's Research UK 2015a) and it has also been associated with improved mental function, such a reduced incidence of depression and improved cognitive function, particularly when carried out in early to midlife (Chang *et al.* 2016; Hoang, *et al.* 2016; Gallaway *et al.*, 2017).

Research has also identified that exercise may have a positive effect on the brain, increasing neural plasticity, flow of blood and oxygen to the brain, increasing synaptic connections and protecting the brain from damage (Cotman and Berchtold 2002; Colcombe *et al.* 2004; Rovio *et al.* 2005).

Rovio *et al*'s (2005) Finnish health and medical history study of 2000 participants reported that those participants who engaged in higher levels of physical activity were less likely to develop a form of dementia. Furthermore, exercise in midlife was associated with a 60 per cent lower risk of developing a form of dementia. Rovio and colleagues also looked at APOE ε4 genetic markers (which have been linked to a increased risk of dementia) within their study, finding that amongst APOE ε4 carriers there was an 'inverse association between midlife physical activity and the subsequent risk of dementia' (p.708), suggesting that a person genetically prone to developing dementia may benefit from exercise to reduce their risk of dementia.

Research by Colcombe *et al.* (2004) adds to the evidence base. Colcombe and colleagues used fitness and oxygen tests with older people living in the community, with no known psychiatric problems or disabilities. They found that exercise can increase the levels of neurochemicals in the brain, help with the development of new neurons, and aid the development of plasticity and synaptic function. Furthermore, higher levels of cardiovascular fitness were associated with improved performance on cognitive tasks. A longitudinal study by Grasset *et al.* (2017) has also found that participation in regular sports could result in living longer without developing dementia.

If studies suggest that physical exercise has a positive impact on health, is there a type of exercise or number of times a person should exercise to gain the most benefit? Rovio *et al.* (2005) suggest twice a week in midlife but add that dementia can be present before any signs are evident and therefore exercising earlier in life will have greater impact. Dementia charities and government policy make recommendations for 30 minutes of moderate-intensity activity five times a week or 15 minutes of high-intensity activity five times a week (Alzheimer's Research UK 2015a). Lautenschlager (2017) makes recommendations for aerobic and strength training exercise for 150 minutes a week. Groot *et al.* (2016) suggest that aerobic activity can have benefits on cognitive function for people who are already diagnosed with dementia. What seems to be clear from the studies is that regular exercise, of moderate to high intensity, can have a positive impact on cognitive function, even if it is not yet known what type or for what duration is optimal (Baumgart *et al.* 2015).

Cognitive activity

The research associated with physical activity found that exercise is not only associated with health benefits but can have a positive impact on mental health and cognitive function. This link with brain function has also been considered with regard to undertaking cognitive activities, as a way of exercising the brain. Early research by Hultsch *et al.* (1999), considers the 'use it or lose it' concept and that engaging in activities which keep the brain active can act as a 'buffer' to later life cognitive decline. However, Midkiff's (2004) longitudinal study of cognitive performance in early, mid and later life, did not find support for this hypothesis, although they do stress that people should not 'discontinue their involvement in cognitively stimulating activities simply because it has not been proven to be an accurate indicator of problem solving abilities' (p.57).

Wang *et al.* (2017) consider that, rather than providing a buffer, engaging in physical, social and cognitive activities can build a reserve over the course of a lifetime to protect against dementia. Their longitudinal study in Sweden studied those over 75 years of age for nine years, collecting data about early, mid and later life activities. An association between taking part in 'reserve-enhancing activities', such as educational attainment, job complexity, and physical, mental and social activity, were associated with a reduced risk of dementia in later life. More importantly, increasing the number of activities engaged in throughout the lifespan was associated with a reduced risk of dementia.

Carlson *et al's* (2008) study of male twins found a 26 per cent reduced risk of dementia for those who were more cognitively and socially active. There was an even higher reduction of risk for those with APOE ε4 gene, at 30 per cent reduced risk for those who were cognitively active. More recently the Cognitive Function and Ageing Study Wales (Clare *et al.* 2017) studied over 2000 individuals aged over 65 years and explored the possible associations between lifestyle, cognitive reserves and the risk of dementia. Cognitive reserves were defined as: number of years in education, nature of employment and job complexity. The study found that modifiable lifestyle factors, such as diet and physical activity, were associated with a reduced risk of dementia in later life. Clare and colleagues also suggest that cognitive reserves are important in building resilience against diseases of the brain. Additionally, these reserves are built up over the course of a lifetime and can fluctuate. They conclude that 'enhancing cognitive reserve throughout the lifespan, and encouraging participation in cognitive, social, and physical activity and a healthy diet, may help maintain cognitive health in later life' (p.12). Both this study and Wang and colleagues' study advocate for not only for the benefit of developing cognitive reserves through early adulthood and the rest of a person's life, but also for a more holistic approach to health, whereby we should be considering our overall physical, mental and social health when we think about preventative factors for dementia.

Alongside the research on cognitive reserves, there has been much discussion on whether targeted training for the brain can be beneficial and can continue to keep the brain active, such as doing puzzles, crosswords etc. Alzheimer's Research UK (2015a) recommend 'keeping mentally active by learning new skills or joining clubs can also be a good way to connect with other people and improve mental wellbeing, helping you to feel happier and more positive in life' (p.15). This recommendation is again erring to a more rounded approach which sees cognitive activities associated with boosting socialisation and wellbeing. But does training the brain support long-term cognitive function?

An early study, ACTIVE (The Advanced Cognitive Training for Independent and Vital Elderly) (Ball *et al.* 2002; Willis *et al.* 2006; Wolinsky *et al.* 2006; Rebok *et al.* 2014) has considered the impact of cognitive training for over ten years. The original study (Ball *et al.* 2002) tested over 2000 individuals over 65 years of age without any sign of cognitive decline. Participants took part in trained ability trials for: memory (mnemonic training to remember lists of words or texts); reasoning (strategies to find the next item in a sequence or identify patterns in letters or words); or speed of processing (training to carry out a visual search while attention was divided between tasks). The training was designed to resemble activities of daily living, such as recalling a telephone number or understanding a bus timetable (Ball *et al.* 2002; Willis *et al.* 2006). Initially, participants were measured at baseline and then after two years, with improvements shown in the tested areas (i.e. reasoning, memory and speed of processing); however, no improvement in overall daily functioning was found (Ball *et al.* 2002).

A follow-up after five years (Willis *et al.* 2006) found similar results to the initial study. However, when compared to the control group, the training groups showed a lower level of decline in everyday functioning, as reported through the Instrumental Activities of Daily Living (IADL). Rebok *et al.* (2014) carried out a ten-year follow-up of the ACTIVE study, supporting earlier findings, that those in the training groups reported less decline in IADL compared to the control group and that training in reasoning and speed of processing could maintain targeted cognitive function over ten years, although training in memory was not found to have been maintained. Rebok and colleagues conclude that targeted cognitive training may have benefits on aspects of cognitive function, potentially delay the onset of dementia and support people to live independently for longer. However, this study had limitations, including attrition rates and type of control group used, which must be taken into consideration when looking at these overall findings (Leshner *et al.* 2017).

Social activity

The evidence discussed supports the need to be both physically and mentally active but has also suggests that a more balanced lifestyle approach is needed, one where we also consider social activities or hobbies as important in addressing risk factors for dementia. NICE (2015) guidance suggests that improving people's resilience through their general wellbeing and mental health can support other aspects of overall health. Reducing a person's risk factors is one way of reducing the likelihood of dementia, but taking preventative measures is also important. One way that people can do this is to engage in social activities, such as maintaining friendships, engaging in hobbies or volunteering. Not only do these activities support general wellbeing but they can also support against loneliness, depression and stress (Public Health England 2016). The way that social engagement can support a person with young onset dementia and their family members is discussed in more detail in Chapter 6.

Other health factors

A number of other health factors are associated with the risk of dementia, primarily hypertension in midlife, smoking, and alcohol consumption. However, depression, diabetes and head injury also have strong associations.

Depression has been reported as a potential risk factor for dementia (Nordström *et al.* 2013; Kar, Singh and Prakash 2015). Richie and colleagues' (2010) study on modifiable risk factors highlights the need to tackle depression, as addressing depression in their cohort reduced the occurrence of dementia by 10 per cent over a seven-year period. The link between depression and dementia is not fully understood, however, recommendations suggest that treatments should focus on early intervention and reduced exposure, particularly for those with a history of dementia in the family (Richie *et al.* 2010). Kar *et al.* (2015) further explore the links between depression and dementia through the neurobiological 'overlap' of both depression and dementia and the similar presentations of both conditions. Changes in serotonin and cortisol levels and inflammation of the cerebral cortex may impact on cognitive function, leading to dementia (Kar *et al.* 2015). The importance of recognising the association between depression and dementia goes beyond identifying depression as a possible risk factor; it should also be acknowledged that it can impact on the way a diagnosis is made, on how the disease progresses and it can add to the burden of care (Kar *et al.* 2015).

Smoking is thought to be a key risk factor for dementia, particularly Alzheimer's disease (Alzheimer's Research UK 2015a; Zhong *et al.* 2015), with Public Health England (2016) stating that it can double the risk of dementia through increased risks from diabetes, stroke and cardiovascular disease. The World Health Organisation estimated that 14 per cent of Alzheimer's disease diagnoses can be attributed to smoking (McKenzie, Bhatti and Tursan d'Espaignet 2014). The NHS (2014) further explains that smoking can result in the narrowing of arteries, which can lead to higher blood pressure and hence put a person at a higher risk of long-term illnesses, including dementia. However, encouraging people to stop smoking can be beneficial, as the cessation of smoking can reduce the risks of dementia to the levels of a non-smoker (Zhong *et al.* 2015).

Increased blood pressure in midlife has been associated as a risk factor for dementia (Iadecola 2014; Peng *et al.* 2017). Hypertension is a risk factor for strokes, which can lead to vascular dementia, however, research also suggests that vascular issues may be connected to Alzheimer's disease (Tzourio 2007; Iadecola 2014). The link with hypertension and cognitive function is explained by Meissner (2016) who states that 'the brain presents an early target for organ damage due to changes in blood pressure' (p.255) which can result in infarcts, microbleeds and white-matter lesions in the brain. Factors already discussed, such as diet, exercise and cessation of smoking, can support the lowering of blood pressure, however, Sierra, Vicario and Escoda (2016) also discuss emergent evidence for the use of medication to control blood pressure and that this may be one way of reducing a person's risk of dementia.

Diabetes is also linked with dementia risk, possibly due to the damage caused by raised sugar levels in the blood. Ciudin *et al.* (2017) found that type 2 diabetes is a risk factor for those with mild cognitive impairment. While, Kar *et al.* (2015) identify that diabetes can result in 'dyslipidemia, increase in pro-inflammatory chemical mediators, decreased insulin sensitivity, alteration in autonomic function, micro-vascular and macro-vascular complications which increases the vulnerability to develop all types of dementia' (p.21). The risk of diabetes, and hence potentially the risk of dementia, can be reduced through improvements to diet and exercise.

Consumption of alcohol in large quantities can have a negative impact on health, blood pressure and cholesterol levels (NHS 2014). A rare form of dementia – Korsakoff's syndrome – is also linked to alcohol-related brain damage, which can develop from years of overuse of alcohol (Alzheimer's Society 2017b). Other types of dementia are also associated with drinking above the recommended limit for alcohol, such as Alzheimer's disease or vascular dementia. Particular risks may be associated with 'binge' and 'heavy' drinking (Alzheimer's Society 2017b). Therefore, government guidance on weekly alcohol consumption should be encouraged and followed.

Head injury may be another risk factor of dementia, although the evidence on this link is not clear. A study by Nordström and colleagues (2014) looked at the association between young onset dementia and traumatic brain injury in Swedish men conscripted into the military with a 30-year follow-up and found that the risk of developing Alzheimer's disease was low for those who had reported incidence of traumatic brain injury. But Shively *et al.* (2012) suggest that traumatic brain injury in mid or early life can be associated with an increased risk of dementia. Furthermore, the association with repeated head injury through sporting activities is also under investigation, particularly sports such as rugby, football and boxing (Alzheimer's Association 2016c). One type of dementia, pugilistica or chronic traumatic encephalopathy (CTE), is thought to be caused by repeated head injury and is often associated with boxing (Shively *et al.* 2012; Alzheimer's Research UK 2015a). Further research is needed to explore these associations and to fully understand the links with dementia.

What has not yet been discussed in this chapter is that singularly these health issues can be a risk for dementia, however, a comorbidity of illness can increase that risk significantly. For example in their study of diabetes and depression, Swardfager and MacIntosh (2017) found that one comorbidity could double the risk of cognitive impairment, but this was increased to triple with two comorbidities. This increased risk is supported by evidence from Nordström *et al.* (2013) who studied young onset dementia in a Swedish cohort study; they who found that risk of developing young onset dementia increased when the participant showed at least two health risk factors, identified as: alcohol use; stroke; antipsychotic drug use; depression; drug use; low cognitive function in early life; hypertension. Many of the risk factors in Nordström and colleagues study were identified as present in adolescence, adding evidence for the need to address health concerns early in life.

Non-modifiable risk factors associated with dementia

As well as the modifiable risk factors associated with dementia, there are also non-modifiable risk factors which should be considered such as: age; gender; ethnicity; and genetics.

Age

Age is the main risk factor for developing dementia, with one in five people aged between 85–89 likely to develop a dementia, compared to two in 100 people aged 65–69 (Alzheimer's Research UK 2015a). With life expectancies increasing and a rise in the number of people living into older age, it is inevitable that there will be a rise in the number of people diagnosed with a dementia (Prince *et al*. 2015). It is not possible to change the ageing process but it is possible, as identified earlier in this chapter, to identify those behaviours and risk factors which can be modified and so reduce a person's risks of developing dementia at a later age.

Gender

Women are at a higher risk of developing dementia. In the UK it is estimated that 65 per cent of those living with dementia are women; it is also the leading cause of death amongst women (Alzheimer's Research 2015b). This may be due to longer life expectancies of women than men and hence the associated risks of ageing and dementia (Erol, Brooker and Peel 2015).

Not only is there a gender difference in developing dementia but also in taking on a caring role within the family. Women tend to take on the caring role, being '2.3 times more likely than men to have been providing care to someone with dementia for more than five years' (Alzheimer's Research 2015b. p.8). Taking on the carer role can have a significant impact on health problems, stress and 'burn-out' and so family carers may require additional support to maintain their health.

Ethnicity

An estimated 40,000 Asian, black and minority ethnic (BAME) people have a diagnosis of dementia in the UK. BAME communities are often diagnosed later in the disease progression and can be under-represented by services (All-Party Parliamentary Group on Dementia 2013).

Some BAME communities may be at a higher risk of some chronic conditions, such as stroke or cardiovascular disease, and as such may be at a higher risk of dementia. In the case of dementia, this may be because dementia awareness and experience of dementia are less common in these communities and can be 'highly stigmatised' (Truswell 2013). Some communities may not even have a word for dementia, so tackling issues of dementia can be complex, and knowing where to access care and support can be limited (Social Care Institute for Excellence (SCIE) 2015). Specific risk factors associated with the BAME communities are stroke, diabetes, hypertension and cardiovascular disease (All-Party Parliamentary Group on Dementia 2013; SCIE 2015), most of which could be tackled through changes in lifestyle such has diet or exercise (Alzheimer's Society 2016a). Raising awareness and a greater understanding of dementia and the associated risk factors should be a priority when working with BAME communities.

Genetics

There is a complex association between genetics and dementia, and young onset dementia is usually linked to rarer forms of dementia. The development of dementia can be the result of a gene mutation or a gene variant. Chapter 2 discusses the rarer forms of dementia, such as Familial Alzheimer's disease, which is caused by a gene mutation which can be passed down through generations of the same family. This form of dementia is particularly associated with young onset, with people developing dementia as early as their 30s (Alzheimer's Society 2016b). Other genetic conditions associated with young onset dementia include Down syndrome and Huntingdon's disease.

Genetic testing is available for people at a high risk of dementia, those with a family history of dementia, particularly those associated with specific genetic markers, such as: Huntington's disease gene (HTT), familial Alzheimer's disease genes (APP, PSEN-1, PSEN-2), and frontotemporal dementia genes (MAPT, GRN and C9ORF72) (Alzheimer's Society 2016b). However, these tests should be accompanied with counselling and only provided for specific cases.

As has been discussed in this chapter, those with higher non-modifiable risk factors such as genes, gender or ethnicity are not predetermined to develop dementia but medical practitioners can work with these groups to look at their modifiable risk factors to reduce any likely risks.

Promotion of health for people living with dementia

Throughout this book the ways in which a person with young onset dementia and their family members can be supported to live better with dementia are discussed, for example through coping strategies, social activities and meaningful engagement in activities (Chapter 6). However, these need to be supported with a healthy physical lifestyle through eating a balanced diet, exercise and sleeping well. Much as these factors are important before a person develops dementia, they are also important after a diagnosis. Barnett *et al.* (2013) identify that poor diet and lack of physical activity can be experienced by people in the early stages of dementia and specific symptoms may be experienced by individuals due to the type of dementia they have. For example, a person with frontotemporal dementia may be prone to increased intake of food due to changes in the brain which impact on their ability to monitor satiety (Mendez, Licht and Shaprira 2008). Medical practitioners should be working with their patients to identify ways in which these healthy lifestyles can be monitored and sustained.

The NHS (NHS 2015) suggests that sleep can be disturbed as a result of medication, stress or symptoms of dementia. The Alzheimer's Society (2017a) also suggest that people with Lewy bodies dementia can have issues with sleeping due to rapid eye movement sleep behaviour disorder, where a person has increased physical movement, hitting, punching, or shouting out. Both the NHS and Alzheimer's Society recommend sleep hygiene measures to support both the person with dementia and family carer, such as limiting daytime naps, maintaining regular sleeping hours and avoiding alcohol or caffeine at night.

Medical practitioners should also consider the needs of those caring for a person with young onset dementia as well as the person living with the diagnosis. Carer burden or burn-out can put additional pressures on health and social services and as such supporting family carers to maintain their health and wellbeing is important. Family carers can experience psychological and physical ill-health (Millenaar *et al.* 2016) and they often have a number of unmet needs, such as: lack of information; loss of feeling valued; stress; lack of time to engage in enjoyable activities; lack of support (Ducharme *et al.* 2014), aspects which health and social care services could support.

Conclusion

Prince *et al.* (2014) reflect that: 'if we can all enter old age with better developed, healthier brains we are likely to live longer, happier and more independent lives with a much reduced chance of developing dementia' (p.5). There is no guarantee that we can prevent dementia but living a healthy and active lifestyle may lower the risk of developing dementia or another serious illness which could develop into dementia, such as a stroke. The research discussed in this chapter makes recommendations for a lifelong consideration of health, particularly as the way we live our lives in the early and middle stages can impact on later life, but also because the effects of dementia begin years before any diagnosis is made (Wang *et al.* 2017). The message from research and policy also emphasises that it is never too late to make a change and that this can impact on the risks of later life dementia.

Risk factors do not mean that someone will develop dementia and conversely that living a healthy, social lifestyle will prevent dementia. However, by following guidance to live well and healthily, there is a greater possibility of not developing dementia or delaying its onset (Alzheimer's Society 2016a). Furthermore being active and healthy is a positive step everyone can take to give themselves a chance of maintaining an independent lifestyle for longer into later life and which medical practitioners can promote through health checks and consultations, particularly for those who may be at a higher risk. Screening for risk factors is high on the agenda, with a trial underway for the inclusion of dementia risk to be included in the NHS Health Checks. Screening can also support identification of those at risk of health problems due to high consumption of alcohol, at risk of diabetes, cardiovascular disease or hypertension (NICE 2015).

High on the policy agenda is the need to raise awareness of the modifiable risk factors associated with dementia and that intervention early in life to change unhealthy lifestyles can reduce the risks, particularly in midlife (NICE 2015). NICE also have a clear message that people who do develop dementia should not be blamed for this, it may not be possible to prevent dementia but reduced risk may result in a delay of onset. Norton *et al.* (2014) recommend more education on modifiable risks.

KEY POINTS

1. As medical practitioners it is important to promote healthy lifestyles and an awareness of the risks and prevention strategies for dementia.

2. Encourage discussion of modifiable risks at health checks.

3. Raise awareness of modifiable risk factors for dementia with those in midlife and provide information about services to support and help people make lifestyle changes.

4. Suggest apps or websites to support health choices and to make changes. The NHS One You is a good starting point.

5. It is never too late to make a change. Changes in midlife can have a positive impact on a person's health and wellbeing and reduce their risk of dementia and other chronic conditions.

References

Albanese, E., Launer, L.J., Egger, M., Prince, M.J., Giannakopoulos, P., Wolters, F.J. and Egan, K. (2017) 'Body mass index in midlife and dementia: Systematic review and meta-regression analysis of 589,649 men and women followed in longitudinal studies.' *Alzheimer's and Dementia: Diagnosis, Assessment and Disease Monitoring 8*, 165–178.

All-Party Parliamentary Group on Dementia (2013) *Dementia does not discriminate: The experiences of black, Asian and minority ethnic communities.* London: House of Commons.

Alzheimer's Research UK (2015a) *Reducing your risk of dementia.* Cambridge: Alzheimer's Research UK.

Alzheimer's Research UK (2015b) *Women and dementia. A marginalised majority.* Cambridge: Alzheimer's Research UK.

Alzheimer's Society (2016a) *Risk factors for dementia. Factsheet 450.* London: Alzheimer's Society.

Alzheimer's Society (2016b) *Genetics of dementia. Factsheet 405.* London: Alzheimer's Society.

Alzheimer's Association (2016c) *Traumatic brain injury (TBI).* America: Alzheimer's Association.

Alzheimer's Society (2017a) *Sleep and night-time disturbance.* London: Alzheimer's Society. Accessed on 07/06/17 at www.alzheimers.org. uk/info/20064/symptoms/107/sleep_and_night-time_disturbance

Alzheimer's Society (2017b) *Alcohol-related brain damage (including Korsakoff's syndrome.* London: Alzheimer's Society. Accessed on 07/06/17 at www.alzheimers.org.uk/info/20007/types_of_ dementia/14/korsakoffs_syndrome_alcohol_related_brain_ damage?gclid=COXD16n03dMCFaK37QodSXsP8Q

Anstey, K. (2017) 'Cognitive and brain ageing – how does diet matter?' *Journal of Nutrition and Intermediary Metabolism 8*, 60–121.

Ball K., Beerch D.B., Helmers K.F., Jobe J.B. *et al.* (2002) 'Effects of cognitive training interventions with older adults.' *Journal of the American Medical Association 288*, 18, 2271–2281.

Baumgart, M., Snyder, H.M., Carrillo, M.C., Fazio, S., Kim, H. and Johns, H. (2015) 'Summary of the evidence on modifiable risk factors for cognitive decline and dementia: A population-based perspective.' *Alzheimer's and Dementia 11*, 718–726.

Barnett, J., Hachinski, V. and Blackwell, A.D. (2013) 'Cognitive health begins at conception: addressing dementia as a lifelong and preventable condition.' *BMC Medicine 11*, 246–252.

Carlson, M.C., Helms, M.J., Steffens, D.C., Burke, J.R., Potter, G.C. and Plassman, B.L. (2008) 'Midlife activity predicts risk of dementia in older male twin pairs.' *Alzheimer's and Dementia 4*, 5, 324–331.

Chang, M., Snaedal, J., Einarsson, B., Bjornsson, S. *et al.* (2016) 'The association between midlife physical activity and depressive symptoms in late life: Age gene/environment susceptibility—Reykjavik study.' *Journals of Gerontology Series A Biological Sciences and Medical Sciences 71*, 4, 502–507.

Ciudin, A., Espinosa, A., Simó-Servant, O., Ruiz, A. *et al.* (2017) 'Type 2 diabetes is an independent risk factor for dementia conversion in patients with mild cognitive impairment.' *Journal of Diabetes and its Complications 31*, 8, 1272–1274.

Clare, L., Wu, Y-T., Teale, J.C., MacLeod, C., Mattews, F., Brayne, C. and Woods, B. (2017) 'Potentially modifiable lifestyle factors, cognitive reserve, and cognitive function in later life: A cross-sectional study.' *PLoS Med 14*, 3, e1002259.

Corrada, M.M., Hayden, K.M., Paganini-Hill, A., Bullain, S.S. *et al.* (2017) 'Age of onset of hypertension and risk of dementia in the oldest-old: The 90+ Study.' *Alzheimer's and Dementia 13*, 2, 103–110.

Cotman, C.W. and Berchtold, N.C. (2002) 'Exercise: A behavioural intervention to enhance brain health and plasticity.' *Trends in Neurosciences 25*, 6, 295–301.

Colcombe, S., Kramer, A.F., Erickson, K.J., Scalf, P. *et al.* (2004) 'Cardiovascular fitness, cortical plasticity, and ageing.' *Proceedings of the National Academy of Sciences of the United States of America 101*, 9, 3316–3321.

Ducharme, F., Kergoat, M-J., Coulombe, R., Lévesque, L., Antoine, P. and Pasquier, F. (2014) 'Unmet support needs of early-onset dementia family caregivers: A mixed-design study.' *BMC Nursing 13*, 49.

Erol, R., Brooker, D. and Peel, E. (2015) *Women and dementia: A Global Research Review*. London: Alzheimer's Disease International.

Gallaway, P.J., Miyake, H., Buchowski, M.J., Shimada, M., Yoshitake, Y., Kim, A.S. and Hongu, N. (2017) 'Physical activity: A viable way to reduce the risks of mild cognitive impairment, Alzheimer's disease, and vascular dementia in older adults.' *Brain Sciences 7*, 22.

Gandy, S., Bartfai, T., Lees, G.V. and Sano, M. (2017) 'Midlife interventions are critical in prevention, delay, or improvement of Alzheimer's disease and vascular cognitive impairment and dementia.' *1000Research 2017 6*, 41.

Grasset, L., Joly, P., Jacqmin-Gadda, H., Letenneur, L. *et al.* (2017) 'Real benefit of a protective factor against dementia: Importance of controlling for death. Example of sport practice.' *PLoS ONE 12*, 4.

Groot, C., Hooghiemstra, A.M., Raijmakers, P.G.H.M., van Berckel, B.N.M. *et al.* (2016) 'The effect of physical activity on cognitive function in patients with dementia: A meta-analysis of randomized control trials.' *Ageing Research Reviews 25*, 13–23.

Hoang, T.D., Reis, J., Zhu, N., Jacobs, D.R. et al. (2016) 'Effect of early adult patterns of physical activity and television viewing on midlife cognitive function.' *JAMA Psychiatry 73*, 73–79.

Hogervorst, E. (2017) 'Healthy lifestyles to prevent dementia and reduce dementia symptoms.' *Working with Older People 21*, 1, 31–39.

Hooghiemstra, A.M., Eggermont, L., Scheltens, P., van der Flier, W.M. *et al.* (2012) 'Study protocol: EXERcise and Cognition In Sedentary adults with Early-ONset dementia (EXERCISE-ON).' *BMC Neurology 12*, 75, 1–8.

Hultsch, D.F., Hertzog, C., Small, B.J. and Dixon, R.A. (1999) 'Use it or lose it: Engaged lifestyle as a buffer of cognitive decline in ageing?' *Psychology and Ageing 14*, 2, 245–263.

Iadecola, C. (2014) 'Hypertension and dementia.' *Hypertension 64*, 3–5.

Kar, S.K., Singh, A. and Prakash, O. (2015) 'Depression in dementia: An update of neurobiologic risk factors.' *Journal of Geriatric Care and Research 2*, 2, 19–25.

Lourida, I., Soni, M., Thompson-Coon, J., Purandare, N., Lang, I.A., Ukoumunne, O.C. and Llewellyn, D.J. (2013) 'Mediterranean diet, cognitive function, and dementia: A systematic review.' *Epidemiology 24*, 4, 479–489.

Lautenschlager, N.T. (2017) *Physical activity and cognitive health. Preventing Dementia. Online MOOC.* Tasmania: University of Tasmania.

Leshner, A., Landis, S., Stroud, C. and Downey, A. (2017) *Preventing Cognitive Decline and Dementia: A Way Forward.* Washington D.C.: The National Academies Of Sciences, Engineering, And Medicine.

Lincoln, P., Fenton, K., Alessi, C., Prince, M. *et al.*. (2014) 'The Blackfriars Consensus on brain health and dementia.' *The Lancet 383*, 1805–1806.

McKenzie, J., Bhatti, L. and Tursan d'Espaignet, E. (2014) *WHO Tobacco Knowledge Summaries: Tobacco and Dementia.* Geneva: World Health Organisation.

Meissner, A. (2016) 'Hypertension and the brain: A risk factor for more than heart disease.' *Cerebrovascular Diseases 42*, 3–4, 255–262.

Mendez, M.F., Licht, E.A. and Shaprira, J.S. (2008) 'Changes in dietary or eating behavior in frontotemporal dementia versus Alzheimer's disease.' *American Journal of Alzheimer's Disease and Other Dementias 23*, 3, 280–285.

Midkiff, K. (2004) 'Use it or lose it? What predicts age-related declines in cognitive performance in elderly adults?' *McNair Scholars Journal 8*, 1, 53–59.

Millenaar, J.K., de Vugt, M.E., Bakker,C., van Vliet,D., Pijnenburg, Y.A., Koopermans, R.T. and Verhey, F.R. (2016) 'The impact of young onset dementia on informal caregivers compared with late onset dementia: Results from the NeedYD study.' *American Journal of Geriatric Psychiatry 24*, 6, 467–474.

Mitchell, S., Ridley, S.H., Sancho, R.M. and Norton, M. (2016) 'The future of dementia risk reduction research: Barriers and solutions.' *Journal of Public Health.* Accessed on 11/10/17 at www.academic.oup.com/jpubhealth/article/doi/10.1093/pubmed/fdw103/3003024/The-future-of-dementia-risk-reduction-research

NHS (2014) *Can dementia be prevented?* London: NHS. Accessed on 07/07/17 at www.nhs.uk/Conditions/dementia-guide/Pages/dementia-prevention.aspx

NHS (2015) Living *well with dementia.* London: NHS. Accessed on 07/07/17 at www.nhs.uk/Conditions/dementia-guide/Pages/living-well-with-dementia.aspx

National Institute for Health and Care Excellence (NICE) (2015) *Dementia, disability and frailty in later life – mid-life approaches to delay or prevent onset.* London: National Institute for Health and Care Excellence.

Nordström, P., Nordström, A., Eriksoon, M., Wahlund, L-O. and Gustafson, Y. (2013) 'Risk factors in late adolescence for young-onset dementia in men a nationwide cohort study.' *JAMA Internal Medicine 173,* 17, 1612–1618.

Nordström, P., Michaëelsson, K., Gustafson, Y. and Nordström, A. (2014) 'Traumatic brain injury and young onset dementia: A nationwide cohort study.' *American Neurological Association,* March, 374–381.

Norton, S., Matthews, F.E., Barnes, D.E., Yaffe, K. and Brayne, C. (2014) 'Potential for primary prevention of Alzheimer's disease: an analysis of population-based data.' *The Lancet Neurology 13,* 8, 788–794.

Peng, M., Chen, G., Tange, K., Campbell, N., Smith, E., Faris, P. and Quan, H. (2017) 'Midlife and late-life blood pressure and vascular dementia: A population based observational study.' *International Journal of Population Data Science 1,* 1, 365.

Prince, M., Albanese, E., Guerchet, M. and Prina, M. (2014) *World Alzheimer Report 2014. Dementia and Risk Reduction – An analysis of protective and modifiable factors.* London: Alzheimer's Disease International.

Prince, M., Wimo, A., Guerchet, M., Ali, G-C., Wu, Y-T. and Prina, M. (2015) *World Alzheimer Report 2015. The Global Impact of Dementia – An analysis of prevalence, incidence, cost and trends.* London: Alzheimer's Disease International.

Public Health England (2016) Health matters: midlife approaches to reduce dementia risk. London: Public Health England. Accessed on 30/04/16 at www.gov.uk/government/publications/health-matters-midlife-approaches-to-reduce-dementia-risk/health-matters-midlife-approaches-to-reduce-dementia-risk

Rebok, G.W., Ball, K., Guey, L.Y., Jones, R.N. *et al.* (2014) 'Ten-year effects of the advanced cognitive training for independent and vital elderly cognitive training trial on cognition and everyday functioning in older adults.' *Journal of American Geriatrics Society 62,* 1, 16–24.

Ritchie, K., Ritchie, C., Berr, C., Artero, S. and Ancelin, M-L. (2010) 'Designing prevention programmes to reduce incidence of dementia: prospective cohort study of modifiable risk factors.' *British Medical Journal 10*, 34, 1–9.

Rovio, S., Kåreholt, I., Helkala, E-L., Winblad, B. *et al.* (2005) 'Leisure-time physical activity at midlife and the risk of dementia and Alzheimer's disease.' *Lancet Neurology 4*, 705–711.

Scarmeas, N., Stern, Y., Tang, M-X., Mayeux, R. and Luchsinger, A.J. (2006) 'Mediterranean diet and risk for Alzheimer's disease.' *Annals of Neurology 59*, 6, 912–921.

Scazufca, M., Menezes, P.R., Araya,R., Di Rienzo, V.D., Almeida, O.P., Gunnell, D. and Lawlor, D.A. (2008) 'Risk factors across the life course and dementia in a Brazilian population: Results from the Sao Paulo Ageing and Health Study (SPAH).' *International Journal of Epidemiology 37*, 4, 879–890.

Social Care Institute for Excellence (SCIE) (2015) *Black and minority ethnic (BME) communities and dementia.* London: SCIE. Accessed on 01/07/17 at www.scie.org.uk/dementia/living-with-dementia/bme

Shively, S., Scher, A., Perl, D.P. and Diaz-Arrastia, R. (2012) 'Dementia resulting from traumatic brain injury: What is the pathology?' *Archives of Neurology 69*, 10, 1245–1251.

Sierra, C., Vicario, A. and Escoda, O. (2016) 'Hypertension, Cognitive Decline, and Dementia.' In A. Coca (ed.) *Hypertension and Brain Damage.* Switzerland: Springer International Publishing.

Srikanth, V. (2017) *Cardiovascular disease, stroke, obesity and dementia risk. Preventing dementia.* Online MOOC. Tasmania: University of Tasmania.

Swardfager, W. and MacIntosh, B.J. (2017) 'Depression, type 2 diabetes, and poststroke cognitive impairment.' *Neurorehabilitation and Neural Repair 31*, 1, 48–55.

Truswell, D. (2013) *Black, Asian and Minority Ethnic Communities and Dementia – Where are we now? A Race Equality Foundation Briefing Paper.* London: Race Equality Foundation.

Tzourio, C. (2007) 'Hypertension, cognitive decline, and dementia: An epidemiological perspective.' *Dialogues in Clinical Neuroscience 9*, 1 61–70.

Wang, H-X., MacDonald, S.W.S., Dekhtyar, S. and Fratiglioni, L. (2017) 'Association of lifelong exposure to cognitive reserve-enhancing factors with dementia risk: A community-based cohort study.' *PLoS Med 14*, 3, e1002251.

Willis S.L., Tennstedt S.L., Marsiske M., Ball K. *et al.* (2006) 'Long-term effects of cognitive training on everyday functional outcomes in older adults.' *Journal of the American Medical Association 296*, 23, 2805–2814.

Wolinsky, F.D., Unverzagt, F.W., Smith, D.M., Jones, R., Wright, E. and Tennstedt, S.L. (2006) 'The effects of the ACTIVE cognitive training trial on clinically relevant declines in health-related quality of life.' *Journal of Gerontology 61B*, 5, 281–287.

Yaffe, K., Barnes, D., Nevitt, M., Lui, L-Y. and Covinsky, K. (2003) 'A prospective study of physical activity and cognitive decline in elderly women. Women who walk.' *Archives of Internal Medicine 161*, 1703–1708.

Zhong, G., Wang, Y., Zhang, Y., Guo, J.J. and Zhao, Y. (2015) 'Smoking is associated with an increased risk of dementia: A meta-analysis of prospective cohort studies with investigation of potential effect modifiers.' *PLOS ONE 10*, 3, 1–23.

CHAPTER 2

Groups at Increased Risk of Young Onset Dementia

Rationale

This chapter will focus on two groups of people who are at increased risk of developing young onset dementia: 1) people who have an intellectual disability and, in particular, Down syndrome; 2) families in which there is a genetic type of dementia. Despite both groups being easily identifiable due to their health profile and family history, there is often a delay in receiving an accurate diagnosis of dementia, and receiving post diagnostic interventions and support. This can lead to inappropriate treatment, increased distress and relationship difficulties.

Learning objectives

The learning objectives for this chapter are to:

- Identify which young onset dementias have a familial link.

- Understand the added stressors families can face when they have a history of genetic dementia within the family.

- Identify how to improve the recognition and diagnosis of young onset dementia in people who have an intellectual disability.

- Recognise the importance of baseline assessment and ongoing screening of people who have Down syndrome.

Introduction

Across all ages, Alzheimer's disease and vascular dementia are the most commonly diagnosed forms of dementia. In those with a diagnosis of dementia who are aged over 65 years of age, around two thirds have a diagnosis of Alzheimer's, as compared with about 34 per cent of people with a diagnosis who are in the under 65 year age group. Vascular dementia rates are broadly similar across all age ranges at about 20 per cent. In addition, younger people diagnosed with dementia are more likely to have frontotemporal dementia, a rarer dementia, genetic or metabolic forms than the older population (Sampson, Warren and Rossor 2004). It has also been suggested that about 10 per cent of cases of dementia diagnosed under the age of 65 years have a genetic cause (Alzheimer's Society 2015).

People with intellectual disabilities are more at risk of developing young onset dementia than the general population at age 60–65 (British Psychological Society and Royal College of Psychiatry 2015). People with Down syndrome are at a higher risk of dementia than others who have an intellectual disability. In Down syndrome this equates to approximately 5–15 per cent of those aged 40–49 years and over, 30 per cent of those aged 50–59 years experiencing significant cognitive decline (McCarron *et al.* 2014) and 80 per cent developing dementia beyond 60 years of age (Wiseman *et al.* 2015).

This chapter aims to explore how dementia can be recognised at an earlier stage in people with an increased risk of young onset dementia, leading to an accurate diagnosis and timely interventions.

Which dementias can have a familial link?

A chromosome is made up of deoxyribonucleic acid (DNA) and protein and they are found tightly coiled in the nucleus of cells. DNA is the hereditary material that is present in a human body. Chromosomes contain many genes that are made up of DNA, and give instructions to make molecules called proteins. Every person has two copies of chromosomes, one inherited from each parent. In total there are 46 chromosomes forming 23 pairs in each cell of our body. It is estimated that around 20,000 different genes are passed from parents to their offspring (Alzheimer's Society 2016). Most genes are the same in all people, but a small number of genes (less than 1 per cent of the total) are slightly different and these small differences contribute to each person's unique physical features.

Current research has identified some rare genetic mutations which cause dementia in the under 65 year age group. These mutations are autosomal dominant, which means that if one parent has a familial type of dementia arising from a genetic mutation, each child has a 50 per cent chance of inheriting this and will then develop the condition later in life, usually in the 30–50 years age range.

Alzheimer's disease

Genetic mutations are found in 7–12 per cent of all cases of young onset Alzheimer's disease (Alzheimer's Society 2015). Familial Alzheimer's disease is rare and is thought to affect approximately 500 families worldwide (Alzheimer's Society 2016).

The genetic mutations leading to familial Alzheimer's disease have been found on:

- Chromosome 21: this genetic mutation is thought lead to an abnormal processing of amyloid precursor protein (APP) and a build-up of protein particles called beta amyloid forming plaques which interfere with the brain cells ability to function effectively.

- Chromosome 14: Presenilin 1 (PSEN-1) abnormalities account for about 80 per cent of all cases of familial Alzheimer's disease (Alzheimer's Society 2016). Almost all PSEN1 gene mutations change single building blocks of DNA and these mutations result in the production of an abnormal PSEN-1 protein. Defective PSEN-1 alters the processing of APP and leads to the overproduction of beta amyloid, which then stick together and build up in the brain, forming clumps called amyloid plaques.

- Chromosome 1: Presenilin 2 (PSEN-2) abnormalities account for less than 5 per cent of all young onset Alzheimer's disease. Two of the most common PSEN-2 mutations that cause early onset Alzheimer's disease change single amino acids used to make PSEN-2. These mutations appear to disrupt the processing of APP, leading to the overproduction of amyloid beta peptide. As in PSEN-1, this protein fragment can build up in the brain and form clumps called amyloid plaques that are characteristic of Alzheimer's disease.

Vascular dementia

Cerebral autosomal dominant arteriopathy with subcortical infarcts and leukoencephalopathy (CADASIL) has been identified as a genetic form of vascular dementia. The genetic mutation occurs on Chromosome 19 and the faulty gene is called NOTCH3, which is a protein that plays a key role in the function and survival of vascular smooth muscle cells. This protein is thought to be essential for the maintenance of blood vessels, including those that supply blood to the brain. There are about 1000 people in the UK affected by CADASIL.

Frontotemporal dementia

In around 20–40 per cent of people with a diagnosis of frontotemporal dementia (FTD) there is evidence of a genetic mutation, with behavioural variant having the highest likelihood of familial transmission (Rohrer *et al.* 2009; Rossor *et al.* 2010). To date there has been limited research into genetic mutation that can lead to FTD but this is likely to develop further in the next few years with more genetic mutations identified. Chromosomes 1, 3, 9 and 17 are currently identified as implicated in genetic mutations in FTD. At present seven genes (C9ORF72, CHMP2B, FUS, GRN (progranulin), MAPT (tau), TARDBP, and VCP) have been associated with familial FTD (Nacmias *et al.* 2013). Three of these genes account for the majority of familial FTD: progranulin (GRN), microtubule associated protein tau (MAPT) and chromosome 9 open reading frame 72 (C9ORF72) (Woolacott and Rohrer 2016). Mutations in the MAPT gene can cause a buildup of a protein called tau, which can damage brain cells and interfere with neuronal communication. C9ORF72 gene mutations can cause FTD or motor neurone disease, a neurological disorder that affects motor neurones and voluntary muscles of the body, in some individuals. The reason for why this presents as FTD or a neurological condition in the same family carrying a genetic mutation is unclear and needs more research.

How can the recognition, diagnosis and interventions for people at increased risk of familial dementia be improved?

Families who have, or are suspected to have, the possibility of a familial dementia may want to know whether they are carrying a genetic mutation to enable them to plan for the future or to be involved in research. In these cases the General Practitioner (GP) should consider referral for genetic counselling and testing. There are two types of genetic testing for single gene mutations:

- Diagnostic genetic testing – for people who have the diagnosis of dementia and who have a strong pattern of family inheritance.

- Predictive genetic testing – to detect genetic patterns and mutations in families who have a high risk of familial dementia.

In both cases a detailed background history needs to be established before genetic counselling and testing takes place. The medical history should ideally span three generations and include finding out the family history of:

- dementia

- organic mental illness (e.g. psychosis)

- neurological conditions (e.g. Parkinson's disease, Motor Neurone Disease).

If any of these are present, then the age at onset of symptoms and age of death should be established. If at all possible the medical notes and/or post mortem records should be examined.

Before genetic testing, the person with the diagnosis of dementia and a family history suggestive of a familial type should be counselled, along with their next of kin. The counselling should include an explanation of the process and the potential implications of the identification of a genetic mutation. Genetic counselling takes place over several months both before and after the genetic testing. The person and their next of kin are also asked whether they want to know the results or want these to be kept on file for access at a later date. Both the person with dementia and their next of kin should consent to proceed with testing.

Finding a genetic mutation predicts that the person will have dementia at some time in their life (unless they die of something else before the genetic mutation is activated) and can pass this to the next generation. The advantages of having a predictive genetic test are that it can remove the uncertainty of not knowing whether the person is carrying the genetic mutation. If families find they have a genetic mutation for familial dementia they can also take this into consideration when planning for the future, or deciding to have children. If a genetic mutation is known, the family should be entitled to pre-implantation genetic diagnosis (PGD), a technique to identify and exclude embryos at risk of carrying the faulty gene. Predictive testing can also enable the person and their family to be involved in research studies into the cause, cure, treatment and care of familial dementia.

There are many disadvantages of knowing that there is a genetic mutation in the family that causes dementia, including the stress of knowing that it is a possibility and watching for signs that the process has started. In addition, the knowledge that as yet there is no known prevention or cure for familial dementia can lead to depression, grief, anger and added stress on a family's relationships. After the genetic counselling most families decide not to proceed with predictive genetic testing.

Some families state that they feel guilty and distressed because they have passed familial dementia onto their children (see Case study 2.1).

CASE STUDY 2.1

Carla's mother was the first to notice small changes in her daughter at the age of 30 years, such as getting lost in familiar places, having difficulty filling out forms and having several small car accidents.

Eventually, Carla was given a diagnosis of familial Alzheimer's disease at the age of 36. Her father had been diagnosed at the age of 37 with the same type of dementia and died six years later aged 43. Other members of Carla's family have also been diagnosed with Alzheimer's disease including her grandfather, her uncle and cousin.

Carla has been living with the effects of dementia for nearly 10 years and is now living in full time care. She has two young children who are now living with their grandmother, and strong family relationships have helped Carla's mother to provide a loving and caring home for her grandchildren. This strong relationship has enabled the family to support each other, the bond between Carla's mother and brother being of particular comfort for both who are living with the second member of their immediate family to be diagnosed with dementia.

Carla's mother talks of her sense of grief at losing her daughter to dementia and how she fears that her daughter is no longer able to recognise her or her children. She also talks of her worry for her son and grandchildren and fear that they may also develop dementia. Members of the family experience, and have to manage, very difficult emotions, often feeling great sadness, guilt and a sense of unfairness about the diagnosis. The family talks of the diagnosis as being 'heart breaking' and having taken a 'massive toll'. For Carla's children there is a sense of loss and they have found it difficult to understand the changes taking place in their mother.

It can be very distressing for the non-affected parent who has watched and cared for their partner with familial dementia, and who now has to watch their child develop the same symptoms that their affected parent had and start the process again. Also, siblings who do not have the genetic mutation can feel guilty that their affected sibling has the faulty gene and not them.

People living with an intellectual disability

Over the last 30 years, the life expectancy of people with an intellectual disability has increased markedly, which has led to an increase in dementia within this population (Bittles and Glasson 2004; British Psychological Society and Royal College of Psychiatry (BPS and RCP) 2015). Dementia can be difficult to diagnose in people with an intellectual disability due to the pre-existing cognitive and functional impairment and also to the way dementia symptoms may be presented in the early stages (BPS and RCP 2015). In addition, often health and social care workers and family carers are not aware of the increased risk of dementia and so do not recognise the early signs, leading to a delay in an accurate diagnosis and appropriate interventions being given (Bittles and Glasson 2004).

Early recognition and diagnosis of dementia in people with an intellectual disability

Early diagnosis and appropriate post diagnostic support and interventions can reduce crises, enable access to specialist services and support, increase quality of life, and enable the person with an intellectual disability to stay in their place of residence longer (Poveda and Broxholme 2016). However, it is important that before a dementia diagnosis is given, other possible reasons for a decline in functional or cognitive, such as depression, physical ill health, sensory impairments, hypothyroidism, medication and life events, environment or routine changes, should be excluded (BPS and RCP 2015).

Dementia screening

As indicated previously, people with Down syndrome are most at risk of developing young onset dementia, with Alzheimer's disease being the most frequently diagnosed (Hartley et al. 2015; Lautarescu, Holland and Zaman 2017). In contrast to the general population the early signs of dementia may present in changes of personality and/or behaviour and a decline in functional ability (Ball et al. 2006; Deb, Hare and Prior 2007; Lautarescu et al. 2017).

In 2008 the Department of Health introduced annual health checks for people with an intellectual disability and these were to be completed by GPs (Department of Health 2009). In 2013/14 NHS England and NHS Employers introduced an opt-in financial incentive scheme for GPs, focused around timely diagnosis of dementia in people who are at increased risk (NHS England and NHS Employers

2013). The GPs who opted-in committed to undertake dementia screens for people with an intellectual disability aged over 50 years and people with Down syndrome over 40 years.

All people living with an intellectual disability, and their family, should be given information on what a dementia screen involves, and the pros and cons of having this, in language that is easy to understand and adapted to the needs of the person to be screened (Rowe 2014). Once agreement is given, then the dementia screening can take place. However it should be recognised that not everyone wants to have a dementia screen and people with an intellectual disability have the same rights as the general population to decline the screen and assessment. For some individuals, and their family, the news of an increased risk of dementia could be too distressing to contemplate (Watchman 2012). Dementia screening can be more effective if it is repeated over a longer period of time to highlight changes, and should ideally take place in the person's own home environment rather than a GP surgery (Evenhuis, Kengen and Eurlings 2007; McCarron *et al.* 2014; BPS and RCP 2015).

If completed in an accurate and timely way, dementia screening provides baseline information with which to compare future results in order to indicate changes suggestive of dementia (Rowe 2014). It is suggested that GPs should screen people with an intellectual disability at the age of 30 years to provide a baseline, and then from the age of 40 years on a two yearly basis and after 50 years annually (BPS and RCP 2015). At the current time there is an absence of appropriate screening tools that can measure the behavioural changes that can specifically indicate the early signs of dementia in people with intellectual disabilities or Down syndrome (Lautarescu *et al.* 2017). However, information can be collected about functional abilities from the person with a disability, the family, care workers (who know the person well) and observation (Fredheim *et al.* 2013). Collecting this information could be a lengthy process if the person's communication abilities are limited or they need adaptations or adjustments.

When a person has an intellectual disability, the early signs of dementia could be missed due to co-morbidity, pre-existing cognitive impairment and the lack of knowledge regarding behavioural and personality changes that could indicate dementia (Rowe 2014). Medical practitioners should work collaboratively with the person and their family, and with intellectual/learning disability services to provide screening and assessment for dementia which could lead to an accurate diagnosis and appropriate post diagnostic interventions and support.

Following a diagnosis of dementia, the needs of the person and their family should be assessed and an appropriate plan of care developed to enable them to live as well as possible, with relevant support and interventions (BPS and RCP 2015). As far as is possible the person should remain in their usual routine, with adaptations and support if necessary.

How can the recognition, diagnosis and interventions for people at increased risk of dementia be improved?

In theory it should be easy to identify families who have an increased risk of familial dementia; however, with more geographical mobility, fragmented families and lack of awareness within families, often medical practitioners, health and social care workers do not know the full family history. Therefore it is not surprising that they do not consider genetic mutations as a possibility when assessing and diagnosing. In addition, often the same genetic mutations may present differently in a family, especially in the case of FTD where dementia or a neurological condition could be diagnosed.

Health and social care professionals should have an awareness of who is at increased risk of familial dementias and how to recognise the early signs, which are not always the same as dementias that occur in the over 65 year age group. In addition health and social care professionals should know how to support the person who is carrying the gene mutation, and their family. Some people may want to have genetic testing to find out whether or not they are carrying the faulty gene, but after genetic counselling may decline the test but continue to be hypervigilant for signs that they have familial dementia, which can lead to depression and anxiety.

Families who have a history of genetic mutation and who have experienced several members of their family presenting with familial dementia often need specialist support to help them deal with the issues and feelings they face. Peer support from other families who have experienced this too can also be very beneficial and help the family feel less alone.

Health and social care professionals and families should be aware of the increased risk of young onset dementia in people with intellectual disabilities and Down syndrome. A baseline should be established and regular screening should take place, especially in the case of Down syndrome, and appropriate interventions put in place.

Conclusion

Some families have an autosomal dominant genetic mutation that can lead to familial dementia. Current research has identified that these genetic mutations can lead to familial forms of Alzheimer's disease, frontotemporal dementia and a form of vascular dementia. Families with these forms of familial dementia have to live with the realisation that there is a risk they too will carry the faulty gene which can cause anxiety, stress, depression and affect their future plans. Non-affected family members can also feel distressed due to fear, guilt and grief.

People with an intellectual disability, and especially Down syndrome, could be at increased risk of young onset dementia. Often an accurate diagnosis is delayed due to families and health and social care professionals not having awareness into the increased risk of dementia.

KEY POINTS

1. Some families are at increased risk of familial dementias due to genetic mutations.

2. Families in which a genetic mutation is present experience a high level of distress, depression, grief and guilt.

3. Genetic counselling and testing is available for at-risk families if they want it, however after the counselling the majority of people decline predicative genetic testing.

4. People with an intellectual disability, and especially Down syndrome, should have a baseline assessment and regular screening due to the increased risk of young onset dementia.

References

Alzheimer's Society (2015) *Younger People with Dementia. Factsheet 440*. London: Alzheimer's Society. Accessed on 01/08/17 at www.alzheimers.org.uk/download/downloads/id/1766/factsheet_what_is_young-onset_dementia.pdf

Alzheimer's Society (2016) *Genetics of Dementia. Factsheet 405*. London: Alzheimer's Society. Accessed on 01/08/17 at www.alzheimers.org.uk/download/downloads/id/1759/factsheet_genetics_of_dementia.pdf

Ball, S.L., Holland, A.J., Huppert, F.A., Treppner, P., Watson, P. and Hon, J. (2006) 'Personality and behaviour changes mark the early stages of Alzheimer's disease in adults with Down's syndrome: Findings from a prospective population-based study.' *International Journal of Geriatric Psychiatry 21*, 661–673.

Bittles, A.H. and Glasson, E.J. (2004) 'Clinical, social and ethical implications of changing life expectancy in Down syndrome.' *Development Medicine and Child Neurology 46*, 4, 282–286.

British Psychological Society and Royal College of Psychiatrists (2015) *Dementia and People with Intellectual Disabilities: Guidance on the assessment, diagnosis, interventions and support of people with intellectual disabilities who develop dementia.* Leicester: BPS.

Deb, S., Hare, M. and Prior, L. (2007) 'Symptoms of dementia among adults with Down syndrome: A qualitative study.' *Journal of Intellectual Disability Research 51*, 726–739.

Department of Health (2009) *Valuing people now: A new three-year strategy for people with learning disabilities. 'Making it happen for everyone.'* London: DH.

Evenhuis, H.M., Kengen, M.F. and Eurlings, H.A.L. (2007) *Dementia questionnaire for people with learning disabilities DLD.* London: Pearson Assessment.

Fredheim, T., Rikard, H.O., Johan, D.L., Kjonsberg, K. and Lien, L. (2013) 'Intellectual disability and mental health problems: A qualitative study of general practitioners' views.' *British Medical Journal 3*, 3.

Hartley, D., Blumenthal, T., Carrillo, M., DiPaolo, G. *et al.* (2015) 'Down syndrome and Alzheimer's disease: Common pathways, common goals.' *Alzheimer's and Dementia 11*, 6, 700–709.

Lautarescu, B.A., Holland, A.J. and Zaman, S.H. (2017) 'The early presentation of dementia in people with Down syndrome: A systematic review of longitudinal studies.' *Neuropsychology Review 27*, 1, 31–45.

McCarron, M., McCallion, P., Reilly, E. and Mulryan, N. (2014) 'A prospective 14 year longitudinal follow-up of dementia in persons with Down syndrome.' *Journal of Intellectual Disability Research 58*, 1, 61–70.

Nacmias, B., Berti, V., Piaceri, I. and Sorbi, S. (2013) 'FDG PET and the genetics of dementia.' *Clinical and Translational Imaging 1*, 4, 235–246.

NHS England and NHS Employers (2013) 2013/14 general medical services (GMS) contract. Guidance and audit requirements for new and amended services. Version 2-2013. England: The NHS Confederation (Employers) Company.

Poveda, B.and Broxholme, S. (2016) 'Assessments for dementia in people with learning disabilities: Evaluation of a dementia battery developed for people with mild to moderate learning disabilities.' *Learning Disability Practice 19*, 1, 31–40.

Rohrer, J.D., Guerreiro, R., Vandrovcova, J., Uphill, J. *etal.* (2009) 'The heritability and genetics of frontotemporal lobar degeneration.' *Neurology 73*, 18, 1451–1456.

Rossor, M.N., Fox, N.C., Mummery, C.J., Schott, J.M. and Warren, J.D. (2010) 'The diagnosis of young onset dementia.' *The Lancet Neurology 9*, 8, 793–806.

Rowe, M. (2014) 'Will General Practitioners be adequately prepared to meet the complexities of enhanced dementia screening for people with learning disabilities and Down syndrome: Key considerations.' *British Journal of Learning Disabilities 44*, 43–48.

Sampson, E.L., Warren, J.D. and Rossor, M.N. (2004) 'Young onset dementia.' *Postgraduate Medical Journal 80*, 125–139.

Watchman, K. (2012) 'People with a learning disability and dementia: Reducing marginalisation.' *Journal of Dementia Care 20*, 34–39.

Wiseman, F.K., Al-Janabi, T., Hardy, J., Karmiloff-Smith, A. *et al.* (2015) 'A genetic cause of Alzheimer disease: Mechanistic insights from Down syndrome.' *Nature reviews. Neuroscience 16*, 9, 564.

Woollacott, I.O. and Rohrer, J.D. (2016) 'The clinical spectrum of sporadic and familial forms of frontotemporal dementia.' *Journal of Neurochemistry 138*, (S1), 6–31.

CHAPTER 3

Why Early Recognition and Diagnosis Matter

Rationale

Early recognition and accurate diagnosis of young onset dementia, combined with appropriate post diagnostic support, can reduce the distress experienced by the whole family, and reduce relationship breakdown (Nicolaou *et al.* 2010; Johannessen and Moller 2011). If a person has a timely diagnosis of dementia it can enable them to actively engage in making plans and decisions about their finances, work, welfare and legal matters (Dening, Jones and Sampson 2011).

Learning objectives

The learning objectives for this chapter are to:

- Understand the importance of the early recognition and accurate diagnosis of young onset dementia.

- Consider why there can be a delay in recognising and diagnosing young onset dementia.

- Identify how to improve the recognition and diagnosis of young onset dementia.

Introduction

Families living with the effects of young onset dementia state that there is a lack of recognition by health and social care services that people under the age of 65 can develop dementia. Early recognition and diagnosis of young onset dementia is important to ensure timely advice, support and intervention can be given to the person diagnosed, and their family in order that they can live as well as possible with the diagnosis (Jefferies and Agrawal 2009).

The early signs and symptoms of young onset dementia can include changes in: concentration; communication; word finding and comprehension; visuospatial ability; personality; behaviour; social functioning; mood; functional abilities; decision making and memory. Early signs of young onset dementia are often insidious in nature and people who are symptomatic, and their family, seek more commonly understood reasons for the changes they have noticed, i.e. stress, relationship difficulties, 'midlife crisis', physical or mental ill health (Johannessen and Moller 2011; Lockeridge and Simpson 2012; Griffin, Oyebode and Allen 2015). As a result there is a substantial delay in seeking a diagnosis, and that can lead to significant family distress and relationship difficulties. It takes young people with dementia on average four years to receive an accurate diagnosis (van Vliet *et al.* 2013), over twice as long as for an older person. In Werner, Stein-Shvachman and Korczyn's (2009) study they found that between 30 and 50 per cent of younger people with dementia were wrongly diagnosed or were given an uncertain diagnosis. Diagnosing young onset dementia requires specialist knowledge and skills due to the variety of different causes and presentations of dementia that affect people under the age of 65 (Rossor *et al.* 2010). Due to the different types and causes of dementia encountered under the age of 65 years, a range of tests and diagnostic procedures will be performed which should include: personal history taking, cognitive tests, blood tests, brain imaging, neurological and physical examination and neuropsychological tests.

It should be noted that not all people with young onset dementia will have memory disturbance as a key feature and it is therefore essential that a careful history is taken, not only from the person with suspected dementia but also from their family. In particular, questions should be asked about the person's behaviour, personality changes, social interactions and everyday living abilities. If possible information about the person's current employment and how they are performing in their job should be obtained.

Once the diagnosis is given, families identify there is a lack of specialist advice and support offered, which further compounds their feelings of distress and isolation. This chapter explores why there may be a delay in recognising and diagnosing young onset dementia, what happens at the time of diagnosis and gives suggestions from families on how this process could be improved.

CASE STUDY 3.1

Families commonly report that the start of young onset dementia is slow and progressive over time, which leads to misunderstandings, changes in relationships, roles and their lifestyle. They know something is wrong but not what it is, and so they often try different approaches to deal with this with no satisfactory results. As the situation gets gradually worse there is recognition that they may need some external intervention, and who they approach depends on what they think is the cause. So for instance the person and their family may seek medical or relationship advice initially. As the symptomatic person, or their family, becomes more concerned, or there is a crisis situation, the symptomatic person, or their family, start to make frequent visits to different people to seek a solution (see Table 3.1).

Table 3.1: The path to diagnosis

Pre diagnosis	Getting a diagnosis
2000 Andrew retired in his 50s and Ann noticed his socially inappropriate behaviour and his lack of interest in people and life in general. *2005–2007* Ann noticed Andrew's inappropriate behaviour was worsening and he was also getting repetitive and forgetful. She considered leaving Andrew. *2007–2010* Ann noticed that Andrew was becoming increasingly obsessive about collecting things. His behaviour towards her was worsening. He had a significant lack of motivation, he was refusing to take care of his personal hygiene and spending large parts of his day doing nothing.	*2010* Ann went to the GP and expressed her concerns over Andrew's behaviour. The GP told her nothing was wrong. *2010* Ann went back to the GP repeatedly with lists of Andrew's behaviour issues causing concern. GP eventually did a memory test and said all was okay. *2010* Ann contacted the GP again, in crisis, and he referred Andrew to a research clinic after Ann's insistence. *2010* Andrew sent for SPECT scan after Ann insists the GP do something. Andrew was given the diagnosis of behavioural variant frontotemporal dementia (bvFTD) at the age of 65 years.

Although Ann knew there were significant issues with Andrew's behaviour and social functioning, she initially attributed this to his retirement, then, as the situation did not improve, to a breakdown in the relationship. After his behaviour towards her became untenable in 2010 and she noticed these changes were progressive in nature, she decided that she needed to approach the medical practitioner for an assessment of Andrew, to seek a diagnosis and treatment. She made many visits to the medical practitioner during 2010 and eventually insisted Andrew was referred for specialist assessment.

Why is there a delay in recognising young onset dementia?

> I kept thinking he was clinically depressed where everything was unbalanced, therefore they would give him medication and everything would become balanced again. Maybe the fact his mum died and he lost his job, maybe these things have caused all this to happen, and maybe these things have been going on for a while for different reasons. I just thought someone was going to make him better. (Spouse, husband symptomatic from 2009 and diagnosed in 2012)

Although families often recognise that there has been a change in a person's behaviour, mood, concentration and cognitive abilities, they tend to attribute this to stress, relationship problems, work issues or depression (Werner *et al.* 2009). There is often a lack of recognition that these changes could be indicative of young onset dementia, unless there is a family history or genetic susceptibility, as the majority of the public think dementia is a disease of old age.

In the early stages of dementia a family, or people close to the symptomatic person, may notice a difference in the person's personality, cognitive ability, communication, functional ability, mood or behaviour, but as the changes are gradual and initially do not significantly affect everyday living they are more likely to be 'explained away' or 'normalised' (Daly *et al.* 2013). When the spouse or partner normalises the behaviour, they tend to make allowances and give extra support for a period of time (Lockeridge and Simpson 2012).

As the dementia progresses and the noticed changes become less easily 'explained away' another reason is sought, which could include mental or physical health issues, life events or relationship breakdown. As these changes become progressively worse and begin to be noticed outside of the family context, families state that they realised medical advice was required:

> Following a social event I got a letter in the post from a friend saying, 'Are you all right because your husband was very odd and everyone said so.' I thought, 'Thank God I'm not the only one who has noticed that he is acting oddly.' I felt relieved it was 'out there' and now I had permission to do something about it. (Spouse, husband symptomatic from 2010 and diagnosed in 2012)

Families often state that they initially felt relief when others noticed the changes and that it gave them permission to act. If they thought that the issues their family member were experiencing could be due to physical or mental health reasons or life events, there was a tendency to persuade them to make an appointment with the medical practitioner for a health check. If the spouse or partner thought it could be due to relationship breakdown they tended to seek help from friends, family or organisations that specialise in relationship breakdown:

> We did go to Relate at one stage to talk about the relationship, that would have been about nine years ago. Actually thinking back to that, he was willing to go and he would talk during the meeting but when we were out he wouldn't talk to me or even try and build on what we talked about. (Spouse, husband symptomatic from 2009 and diagnosed in 2012)

If the spouse or partner initially attributed their partner's behaviour to relationship breakdown, they often assumed that the person was intentionally behaving differently and hurtfully towards them, which created misunderstandings, arguments and resentment. Massimo, Evans and Benner (2013) noted that changes that can occur as a result of dementia can lead to a growing state of dependence which can lead to a change in role for the unaffected spouse/partner, from partner to carer. This process was identified as difficult for the non-affected spouse, and is frequently accompanied by feelings of isolation, anger and grief.

Insight into the changes experienced by the symptomatic person can be very variable depending on the type of dementia and which areas of the brain are affected. It is not just the spouse or partner that 'explains away or normalises' the changes, this can also be exhibited by the person who has the symptoms of young onset dementia. In addition, there is often a misconception that dementia only occurs in old age so the family and others do not recognise the signs and symptoms at an early stage.

Getting an accurate diagnosis

Diagnostic difficulties can occur due to the rarity of dementia in people under the age of 65 years as compared to the over 65 year age group (Rossor *et al.* 2010) and the gradual changes over time (Liebson *et al.* 2005). The diagnostic process can be characterised by repeated visits to the doctor's to get a diagnosis, with increasing levels of distress and frustration at not being listened to:

> When I went back I went with a list and I had this list in front of me. When he (the GP) started questioning me I said, 'I will take questions at the end and want

to have my say first and I want you to listen to what
I have to say.' (Spouse, husband symptomatic from
2000 and diagnosed in 2010)

In addition to the distress families experience trying to get a diagnosis, if they are then initially given a wrong diagnosis it can lead to feelings of hope, especially if their family member is misdiagnosed with a treatable or potentially curable condition. This can lead to additional distress when the family realise that the initial diagnosis is incorrect, and their hopes of returning to normal are dashed. This can lead to a delay in diagnosis, with families potentially experiencing further changes to their familial and social relationships.

Delays in diagnosis may occur due to medical practitioner's lack of awareness, specialist knowledge, skills and experience regarding young onset dementia (Johannessen and Moller 2011; Cabote, Bramble and McCann 2015). Misdiagnosis or diagnostic delays can also occur due to the medical practitioner not involving the family in the diagnostic process or listening to their concerns (Johannessen and Moller 2011). As previously identified, if the symptomatic person is not aware they are experiencing the changes associated with young onset dementia, are frightened or are in denial about the signs and symptoms, they may deny they have problems or 'explain them away' (Clare 2003; Rascovsky et al. 2011; Stephan and Brayne 2014).

As identified previously, families often significantly delay approaching a medical practitioner in the belief that things will improve over time, and when they do present for a consultation it is often as a result of a stressful situation or crisis (Chow, Pio, and Rockwood 2011; Lockeridge and Simpson 2012). The consultation may be characterised by a difference of opinion between the attendees of the extent of the changes and the effects on their lives, especially if insight into the condition has been affected. At this point it could mistakenly be perceived that it is relationship breakdown or mental health issue that is present rather than young onset dementia.

Families should not have to fight to get the correct diagnosis as they are already experiencing a significant degree of concern, distress, fear and worry. In addition, they may have significant changes to their lifestyle, relationship and roles, which will also add to their pressure.

How can the recognition and diagnosis of young onset dementia be improved?

Medical practitioners should listen to the family's concerns, as they are able to give a first-hand experience of the changes experienced in their family member (Manoochehri and Huey 2012; Pressman and Miller 2014). One way of encouraging this would be to suggest that the spouse, partner or family write down a bullet point list of what the change is, when it occurs, how frequently, the context and how it affects the person's and family's life. This could be submitted before the consultation so that it is available to the medical practitioner before the appointment to aid in providing important information that could aid the diagnostic process.

Families who are living with the effects of young onset dementia suggest that in addition to the use of a submitted list of concerns, they should also be actively involved in appointments and decision-making regarding treatment and care with the symptomatic person.

Training is needed for all health, social care, agency and voluntary organisation staff regarding the early recognition and accurate diagnosis of young onset dementia. In addition, there needs to be a national awareness campaign for the general public of the signs and symptoms of young onset dementia, as frequently there is a significant delay in the symptomatic person and their family recognising the signs and symptoms. This can lead to a delay in presenting to medical practitioners for an assessment, diagnosis and appropriate post diagnostic interventions and support.

Medical practitioners need a clear referral pathway indicating who and how to refer a person who has the symptoms of young onset dementia.[1] People who are symptomatic of young onset dementia should be referred to a specialist in assessment and diagnosis of young onset and rare dementias, as they are more likely to have the experience, specialist knowledge and skills to make an accurate diagnosis in a timely way.

Conclusion

Recognition and subsequent diagnosis of young onset dementia can be affected by lack of awareness that people under 65 years can have dementia. It can also be due to attributing early signs and symptoms to other potential causes, i.e. mental or physical health issues, stress or relationship breakdown. In addition, the symptomatic person may be in denial or lack insight about the changes or be frightened of the implications. The early recognition and accurate diagnosis of young onset dementia is important to ensure that the person and their family are aware what has caused the changes experienced and are able to consider how they can work together to maintain their lifestyle, roles and relationships. Early recognition and accurate diagnosis could be improved by awareness raising for health and social care professionals and the general public regarding

---

1   For an example of a GP referral pathway see www.youngdementiauk.org/gp-decision-making-tool

young onset dementia. Once the symptoms are recognised, an appropriate referral should be made to a specialist in assessing and diagnosing young onset and rare dementias.

KEY POINTS

1. People who are symptomatic of young onset dementia may not be aware of, or may be in denial about, the changes in their cognitive functioning, everyday ability, behaviour or personality. It is important to seek the views of the spouse, partner or family.

2. Refer people with suspected young onset dementia to a specialist in the assessment and diagnosis of young onset and rare dementias.

3. When given the diagnosis, the person and their family should also be given appropriate advice regarding what help and support they can receive.

References

Cabote, C.J., Bramble, M. and McCann, D. (2015) 'Family caregivers' experiences of caring for a relative with younger onset dementia: A qualitative systematic review.' *Journal of Family Nursing 21,* 3, 443–468.

Chow, T.W., Pio, F.J. and Rockwood, K. (2011) 'An international needs assessment of caregivers for frontotemporal dementia.' *Canadian Journal of Neurological Sciences 38,* 753–757.

Clare, L. (2003) 'Managing threats to self: awareness in early stage Alzheimer's disease.' *Social Science and Medicine 57,* 1017–1029.

Daly, L., McCarron, M., Higgins, A. and McCallion, P. (2013) '"Sustaining Place"- a grounded theory of how informal carers of people with dementia manage alterations to relationships within their social worlds.' *Journal of Clinical Nursing 22,* 501–512.

Dening, K.H., Jones, L. and Sampson, E.L. (2011) 'Advance care planning for people with dementia: A review.' *International Psychogeriatrics 23,* 10, 1535–1551.

Griffin, J., Oyebode, J.R. and Allen, J. (2015) 'Living with a diagnosis of behavioural variant frontotemporal dementia: The person's experience.' *Dementia 15*, 6, 1622–1642.

Jefferies, K. and Agrawal, N. (2009) 'Early onset dementia.' *Advances in Psychiatric Treatment 15*, 5, 380–388.

Johannessen, A. and Moller, A.(2011) 'Experiences of persons with early onset dementia in everyday life: A qualitative study.' *Dementia 12*, 4, 410–424.

Liebson, E., Rauch, P., Graff, S. and Folstein, M. (2005) 'Early onset dementia: Diagnostic considerations and implications for families.' *Harvard Review of Psychiatry 13*, 102–111.

Lockeridge, S. and Simpson, J. (2012) 'The experience of caring for a partner with young onset dementia: How younger carers cope.' *Dementia 12*, 5, 635–651.

Manoochehri, M. and Huey, E.D. (2012) 'Diagnosis and management of behavioral issues in frontotemporal dementia.' *Current Neurology and Neuroscience Reports 12*, 5, 528–536.

Massimo, L., Evans, L.K. and Benner, P. (2013) 'Caring for loved ones with frontotemporal degeneration: The lived experiences of spouses.' *Geriatric Nursing 34*, 302–306.

Nicolaou, P., Egan, S.J., Gasson, N. and Kane, R. (2010) 'Identifying needs, burden and distress of carers of people with frontotemporal dementia compared to Alzheimer's disease.' *Dementia 9*, 2, 215–235.

Pressman, P.S. and Miller, B.L. (2014) 'Diagnosis and management of behavioural variant frontotemporal dementia.' *Biological Psychiatry 75*, 574–581.

Rascovsky, K., Hodges, J.R., Knopman, D., Mendez, M.F. *et al.* (2011) 'Sensitivity of revised diagnostic criteria for the behavioural variant of frontotemporal dementia.' *Brain: A Journal of Neurology 134*, Pt 9, 2456–2477.

Rossor, M.N., Fox, N.C., Mummery, C.J., Schott, J.M. and Warren, J.D. (2010) 'The diagnosis of young onset dementia.' *The Lancet Neurology 9*, 8, 793–806.

Stephan, B. and Brayne, C. (2014) 'Prevalence and Projections of Dementia.' In M. Downs and B. Bowers (eds) *Excellence in Dementia Care: Research into Practice (2nd edition)*.Berkshire: Open University Press.

Van Vliet, D., de Vugt, M.E., Bakker, C., Pijnenburg, Y.A.L., Vernooij-Dassen, M.J.F.J., Koopmans, R.T.C.M. and Verhey, F.R.J.(2013) 'Time to diagnosis in young onset dementia as compared with late onset dementia.' *Psychological Medicine 43*, 2, 423–432.

Werner, P., Stein-Shvachman, I. and Korczyn, A.D. (2009) 'Early onset dementia: Clinical and social aspects.' *International Psychogeriatrics 21*, 4, 631–636.

CHAPTER 4

Post Diagnostic Support and Intervention

Rationale

Families expect that once a diagnosis of young onset dementia is given they will receive advice about what treatment and support they will be able to access. However, a survey by the Alzheimer's Society (2014) revealed that 43 per cent of family carers and 52 per cent of people living with dementia did not believe they received enough support after diagnosis. Although this survey explored the views of people across the age range of dementia, it could be argued that the situation for younger people diagnosed with dementia is likely to be worse for a variety of reasons, including delay in the recognition and diagnosis of young onset dementia, lack of expertise, and a scarcity of appropriate services and support. Timely post diagnostic support is important for the person with the diagnosis and their family, in order for them to develop an understanding of what the diagnosis means for them and how they will manage this, and to assist them to make decisions about the future and find out what help is available.

Learning objectives

The learning objectives for this chapter are to:

- Understand the importance of timely post diagnostic support and interventions for the person diagnosed with young onset dementia, and their family.

- Explore why there can be a delay in receiving timely post diagnostic support and interventions.

- Examine how post diagnostic support and interventions can be improved for people living with a diagnosis of young onset dementia and their family

Introduction

There is a tendency for services and support to be developed for the needs of older people as dementia is more prevalent in the over 65 year age group (Beattie *et al.* 2004). This has resulted in services and support that do not adequately meet the identified needs of people living with young onset dementia or their families (Armari, Jarmolowicz and Panegyres 2013; Carter, Oyebode and Koopmans 2017; Cations *et al.* 2017).

Younger people living with dementia and their families are more likely to have a rarer dementia, experience a longer wait for an accurate diagnosis, have a younger family who may be financially dependent, and be in, or have recently left, employment. These issues are less likely to occur in people over the age of 65 years and hence services and support tend not to address them. For families living with young onset dementia these issues can cause significant family distress and social isolation (Lockeridge and Simpson 2012), especially if they do not receive timely, and appropriate, post diagnostic support and interventions. Across the UK, and internationally, there is a widespread variation in giving timely post diagnostic support and interventions (Fortinsky *et al.* 2010; Koch and Illiffe 2011; Brooker *et al.* 2014).

The need for specialist advice and support to reduce family distress for the person living with dementia, and their family, has been identified in studies (Johannessen and Moller 2011; Lockeridge and Simpson 2012; Diehl-Schmid *et al.* 2013; Kaiser and Panegyres 2007; see Box 4.1).

Box 4.1: The goals of post diagnostic support

1. Increase a family's knowledge and understanding of dementia to help them develop preventative and coping techniques in managing dementia related cognitive and behavioural issues.

2. Sustain and improve the psychological and physical health of the family.

3. Develop person- and family-centred plans.

4. Maximise independence of the person living with dementia by developing strengths-based approaches and meaningful activity.

5. Identify the family's need for respite and support.

6. Avoid or delay inappropriate admissions to hospital or long-term care.

7. Introduce the concept of peer support.

8. Identify any interest in taking part in research studies or service development.

9. Provide a consistent contact point for the family.

At the time of diagnosis families can feel disappointed, angry, abandoned and trapped by the situation they find themselves in, especially if they do not receive timely post diagnostic support and interventions (Werner, Stein-Shvachman and Korczyn 2009; Lockeridge and Simpson 2012; Armari *et al.* 2013). In the absence of timely post diagnostic advice and interventions families attempt to seek out information and support themselves, which can add to their distress (Johannessen and Moller 2011).

This chapter explores the importance of timely post diagnostic support and interventions, considers why there may be a delay in receiving it, and make suggestions about how this process could be improved (see Case study 4.1 below).

CASE STUDY 4.1

After being made redundant from his job in 2008, Brian set up a consultancy business. All was going well until 2010 when Betty first noticed that Brian was getting confused about where he was going and his communication with family and friends started to significantly reduce. In 2010/11 Brian became repetitive and obsessive over finances and started to make unwise decisions in his work and with family finances. In 2012, after several visits to the GP, he was diagnosed with dementia and Betty reports that she received no post diagnostic advice and support.

In 2013 Betty went back to the GP and asked for support and they were referred to a social worker. When they were seen by the social worker they were instructed to seek out services themselves if they were self funding, with no guidance or follow up. As Betty is in employment and she worried when Brian was left alone at home all day, she booked him into a day centre who stated they would be able to meet his needs. Unfortunately after he attended there the first time they stated they could not 'cope with him' and signposted them to two other day centres who could offer support. Both of these centres stated they could not meet Brian's needs and so Betty had to arrange a private carer to visit him three times per day on the days she works. She was not happy with the arrangement but felt she had no other option and really did not want to give up work.

Brian and Betty thought that once the correct diagnosis was given they would automatically receive the help and support they needed. However, this was not the case and they found that some services which were eventually recommended, could not meet Brian's needs. The lack of services can lead to the partner of the person diagnosed having to give up their own employment and interests in order to manage the home situation.

Why is it important to receive timely post diagnostic support and interventions?

> That summer after the diagnosis was the worst time as we had no support whatsoever, no one to ask, no one to go to, I didn't know what to do. I spent a lot of that summer crying. This time, as well as pre diagnosis, is when you need someone and there just wasn't anyone! Seven months after the diagnosis the GP referred us to the Mental Health Team. (Spouse diagnosed in 2010, received post diagnostic support 2011)

Prior to the diagnosis, families report feeling distressed as they search for a reason why their family member is changing, and there is an expectation that once a diagnosis is made treatment and support will be given. If this does not happen, families report feeling a relationship and role conflict with associated stress and frustration (Svanberg, Stott and Spector 2010).

> I asked a GP what could I expect and he said, 'Very little.' We did finally see someone after 18 months and I was, 'Oh at last.' They came around and spent about two hours with me, I thought, 'Thank goodness, I've got somebody', then they left and I never saw them again. Six months passed by and another person visited, and then nothing, and then another person visited. I got to the point I wasn't even going to bother with them, they were so useless. (Spouse diagnosed in 2012, received post diagnostic support 2013)

It has been established that younger people living with dementia and their families can have a greater need for emotional, psychological and relationship support as compared to older people (Nicolaou *et al.* 2010; Johannessen and Moller 2011), especially if there are changes in personality, behaviour and social functioning (Nicolaou *et al.* 2010; Mioshi *et al.* 2013). Post diagnostic support and interventions can help families to adapt to the changes in roles, relationships and everyday living abilities (Kipps, Mioshi and Hodges 2009; Nicolaou *et al.* 2010; Daly *et al.* 2013; Mioshi *et al.* 2013).

Families often voice an overwhelming sense of sadness and grief when they realise that a family member has a diagnosis that is not only life limiting but can have major effects on their life together.

> Sometimes it hits me when I am out and about and I think this is all a bit superficial. Now I've got this sad

space because I've lost my soul mate and the future we thought we would have. (Spouse diagnosed in 2012, received post diagnostic support 2013)

It is an ugly, ugly illness. I wish I had a pound for every time I thought 'I wish she had cancer.' (Mother of daughter who was diagnosed in 2012)

There can be a realisation that previous hopes and aspirations may need to be revised (Evans and Lee 2014). Families living with the effects of dementia can experience anticipatory grief (Chan *et al.* 2013) due to the multiple losses that can occur after diagnosis. Evans and Lee (2014) wrote about the 'loss of person within', where the person with a diagnosis looks the same but they are no longer who they were. Families can find this particularly hard to cope with, and often because the person still looks the way they did before other people external to the family do not recognise that the family needs their support and understanding.

Because he looks 'normal' and he is quiet I don't think people realise he has a problem. I don't think people understand his wife's situation. He needs someone with him 24 hours a day. (Family friend of a spouse whose husband was diagnosed in 2012)

The media has a tendency to focus on the negatives of dementia with a message of 'No cure, no hope and no help' (Litherland and Capstick 2011). This can lead to discrimination and stigma not just for the person living with the diagnosis but also their family. It can result in the family not sharing the diagnosis with others in their local community. This can be due to embarrassment or worry about how other people will respond to the diagnosis, and this can also be seen in children of parents with a diagnosis of dementia (van Vliet *et al.* 2010; Oyebode, Bradley and Allen 2013; Hutchinson *et al.* 2014).

> I try to avoid telling people what the issues are. I haven't been to the local shop to speak with them. I think I have avoided the embarrassment of going there. (Spouse diagnosed in 2012, received post diagnostic support 2013)

This can lead to a lack of awareness of the issues that the person living with the diagnosis and their family face on a daily basis. It could also limit the amount of support that is offered by the local community. This can lead to feelings of abandonment and other people's lack of understanding can increase stress and burden for the family (Riedijk *et al.* 2006; Lockeridge and Simpson 2012). Nay *et al.* (2015) noted that families are more likely to experience social exclusion, isolation and stress and there is a need for social participation and carer support. There is a need for timely post diagnostic support and interventions focusing on retaining and developing family links with local community family and friends.

> Even my own mother who sees it from the inside because she stays with us, finds it difficult to accept what is happening. I find this very upsetting. They seem to play it down or not comprehend how this must be for me trying to work, run a house, raise a family and becoming a carer. (Spouse diagnosed in 2012, received post diagnostic support 2013)

Relationship and role changes within the family can be particularly difficult to cope with, especially where there have been competing demands and lack of control over the situation the family finds itself in (Baikie 2002; Svanberg *et al.* 2010). The reasons given for the distress include: lack of information and support (Denny *et al.* 2012); grief and loss (Svanberg *et al.* 2010; Denny *et al.* 2012); social isolation due to embarrassment (Hutchinson *et al.* 2014); and behaviour and personality change of parent (Denny *et al.* 2012). Loss of intimate exchange also contributes to role overload and depressive symptoms (Adams, McClendon and Smyth 2008).

People living with a diagnosis of dementia and their families can also make adaptations to their lives to maintain roles, relationships and meaningful activities.

> This is the happiest I have ever known him. He is content with life. (Spouse regarding her husband who is receiving appropriate post diagnostic services and support)

This can be due to the end of uncertainty about why a family member is changing, especially when post diagnostic support and interventions are put in place that focus on the strengths of the individual and establish meaningful activities and social networks, support and connectedness to others. Indeed, some people who have received the diagnosis get actively involved in awareness raising and campaigning which can challenge some of the myths and stereotypes of dementia and also make recommendations on how to improve services and support. However it should also be noted that some people living with the diagnosis and their family can also be negatively affected by the media's and charities portrayal of the more positive viewpoint of living with dementia, 'Living well with dementia'. They may compare their experience with what is portrayed and feel distress, a sense of betrayal or inadequacy that their experience is so different.

If families are offered post diagnostic support and interventions to help them adapt to the diagnosis and the changes that can develop, with a focus on strengths and what the person can do rather than the deficits, it can help families work together to live as well as possible with dementia.

Why could there be a delay in receiving post diagnostic support and interventions?

There is a widespread variation in giving appropriate post diagnostic support and interventions (Fortinsky *et al.* 2010; Koch and Iliffe 2011; Carter *et al.* 2017; Cations *et al.* 2017). Delays in receiving post diagnostic support and intervention could occur due to a lack of specialist services and support in a geographical area. There has been a widespread reduction in funding to health and social care which has resulted in some specialist younger onset dementia services being reduced or cut entirely, in the mistaken believe that generic dementia services can meet every person's needs.

> I visited two centres around here on the recommendations of social services. It turns out one of those doesn't accept people with dementia. So I had to accept the other one. The bus came and he got on and went to the centre from 10–2pm. He went a few times but then the social worker contacted me to say the centre believed they were unsuitable for my husband because of his behaviour and age. There is another centre but it is quite a way away and is more expensive at £50 per day for 10–2pm. (Spouse diagnosed in 2012, received post diagnostic support 2014)

As young onset dementia assessment and diagnosis can be a complex process due to the unusual presentations and rarer conditions, often people are referred to regional or national centres for diagnosis. The staff within these centres are understandably not as aware of what support and interventions are on offer in the person's local area and so rely on the person's medical practitioner to signpost and refer the person with the diagnosis and their family to relevant services for support. This is a time when families report they 'fall through the net' due to a communication breakdown.

How can post diagnostic support and interventions be improved?

Although there has been a growing focus on developing community awareness of dementia in the UK (e.g. dementia friends, dementia friendly communities and dementia friendly businesses) the specialist needs of younger people living with the effects of dementia and their families have not been adequately addressed (Carter *et al.* 2017; Cations *et al.* 2017). The aspirations identified in the Prime Minister's Challenge on Dementia 2020 (Department of Health 2015) largely focus on research and building community awareness; whilst this is laudable and will lead to some positive changes for dementia in general, without adequate funding they will not be able to progress to reality. In addition, there has been comparatively little focus on or funding commitments for post diagnostic support and interventions for people diagnosed with dementia across the age range. There were no specific commitments on developing specialist post diagnostic support for younger people diagnosed with dementia and their families. Future policy development regarding dementia should include the need for specialist post diagnostic support and should actively consult and involve younger people living with the effects of dementia and their families to ensure what is proposed and delivered meet the identified needs (Mayrhofer *et al.* 2017).

Families participating in research studies into young onset dementia state that post diagnostic support should be delivered by health and social care staff who have specialist knowledge and skills. People living with a diagnosis of young onset dementia and their families indicated that this specialist post diagnostic support and interventions are needed to enable them to understand what is happening to their family member, to develop coping strategies (Nicolaou *et al.* 2010; Lockeridge and Simpson 2012), to retain relationships (Hellstrom, Nolan and Lundh 2007; Lockeridge and Simpson 2012; La Fontaine and Oyebode 2014) and social connectedness (Harris and Keady 2009; Barlett and O'Connor 2010; Johannessen and Moller 2011; Lockeridge and Simpson 2012).

People living with a diagnosis of dementia, and their families, identify that they would prefer meaningful activities which are enjoyable, focused on the strengths of the person diagnosed, and can develop new interests or skills (Doherty *et al.* 2009; Peel and Harding 2013; Nay *et al.* 2015). Families of people who are diagnosed with young onset dementia state that they would appreciate peer group support, so they can meet with other families who are having a similar experience, so they do not feel so isolated and can pick up techniques and approaches that have worked for others when facing a difficult issue or decision. Cations and colleagues (2017) recommend that services for people living with a diagnosis of young onset dementia should be designed especially for the needs of younger people and be tailored to the needs of the person with dementia and their family. They also state that services should be flexible, affordable and meaningful. They also recommend that ideally families should have an identified key worker or case manager, which is something that the Young Dementia Network identifies as best practice (Carter *et al.* 2017).

Conclusion

Younger people living with the effects of dementia and their families have a greater need for emotional, psychological and relationship work than people diagnosed later in life. Timely post diagnostic support and interventions can help families adapt to changes in abilities, relationships and roles. Post diagnostic support is important for families living with the effects of young onset dementia to enable them to understand what the diagnosis means for the whole family and to make the necessary adjustments, develop plans and coping strategies to deal with any issues that may arise. Families living with the effects of young onset dementia indicate that they need an identified knowledgeable professional to provide continuity, guidance and support throughout their journey after a member has been diagnosed with young onset dementia.

KEY POINTS

1. Specialist post diagnostic support and interventions should be offered at the time of diagnosis.

2. The person diagnosed with young onset dementia and their family should be actively involved in planning interventions and support that meets their needs.

3. Interventions and support plans should be focused on meaningful activity and maintaining and developing social connectedness and citizenship.

References

Adams, K.B., McClendon, M.J. and Smyth, K.A. (2008) 'Personal losses and relationship quality in dementia care giving.' *Dementia 7,* 301.

Alzheimer's Society (2014) *Dementia 2014: Opportunity for Change.* London: Alzheimer's Society.

Armari, E., Jarmolowicz, A. and Panegyres, P.K. (2013) 'The needs of patients with early onset dementia.' *American Journal of Alzheimer's Disease and Other Dementias 28,* 1, 42–46.

Baikie, E. (2002) 'The impact of dementia on marital relationships.' *Sexual and Relationship Therapy 17,* 3, 289–299.

Bartlett, R. and O'Connor, D. (2010) *Broadening the Dementia Debate: Towards Social Citizenship.* Bristol: The Policy Press.

Beattie, A., Daker-White, G., Gilliard, J. and Means, R. (2004) '"How can they tell?" A qualitative study of the views of younger people about their dementia and dementia care services.' *Health and Social Care in the Community 12,* 4, 359–368.

Brooker, D., La Fontaine, J., Evans, S., Bray, J. and Saad, K. (2014) 'Public health guidance to facilitate timely diagnosis of dementia: Alzheimer's Cooperative Valuation in Europe Recommendations.' *International Journal of Geriatric Psychiatry 29,* 682–693.

Cations, M., Withall, A., Horsfall, R., Denham, N. *et al.* (2017) 'Why aren't people with young onset dementia and their supporters using formal services? Results from the INSPIRED study.' *PloS one 12,* 7, e0180935.

Carter, J.E., Oyebode, J.R. and Koopmans, R.T.C.M. (2017) 'Young-onset dementia and the need for specialist care: A national and international perspective.' *Aging and Mental Health.* Accessed on 16/10/17 at www.tandf online.com/doi/pdf/10.1080/13607863.2016.1257563?need Access=true&

Chan, D., Livingstone, G., Jones, L. and Sampson, E.L. (2013) 'Grief reactions in dementia carers: A systematic review.' *International Journal of Geriatric Psychiatry 28,* 1, 1–17.

Daly, L., McCarron, M., Higgins, A. and McCallion, P. (2013) '"Sustaining Place" – a grounded theory of how informal carers of people with dementia manage alterations to relationships within their social worlds.' *Journal of Clinical Nursing 22,* 501–512.

Denny, S.S., Morhardt, D., Gaul, J.E., Lester, P., Andersen, G., Higgins, P.J. and Nee, L. (2012) 'Caring for children of parents with frontotemporal degeneration: A report of the AFTD task force on families with children.' *American Journal of Alzheimer's Disease and Other Dementias 27,* 8, 568–578.

Department of Health (2015) Prime Minister's Challenge on Dementia 2020. London: DH.

Diehl-Schmid, J., Schmidt, E-M., Nunnemann, S., Riedl, L. *et al.* (2013) 'Caregiver burden and needs in frontotemporal dementia.' *Journal of Geriatric Psychiatry 26*, 4, 221–229.

Doherty, D., Benbow, S.M., Craig, J. and Smith, C. (2009) 'Patients' and carers' journeys through older people's mental health services: Powerful tools for learning.' *Dementia 8*, 4, 501–513.

Evans, D. and Lee, E. (2014) 'Impact of dementia on marriage: A qualitative systematic review.' *Dementia 13*, 3, 330–349.

Fortinsky, R.H., Zlateva, I., Delaney, C. and Kleppinger, A. (2010) 'Primary care physician's dementia care practices: Evidence of geographic variation.' *The Gerontologist 50*, 179–191.

Harris, P.B. and Keady, J. (2009) 'Selfhood in younger onset dementia: Transitions and testimonies.' *Aging and Mental Health 13*, 3, 437–444.

Hellstrom, I., Nolan, M. and Lundh, U. (2007) 'Sustaining "couplehood".' *Dementia 6*, 3, 383–409.

Hutchinson, K., Roberts, C., Kurrie, S. and Daly, M. (2014) 'The emotional well-being of young people having a parent with young onset dementia.' *Dementia 15*, 4, 609–628.

Johannessen, A. and Moller, A. (2011) 'Experiences of persons with early onset dementia in everyday life: A qualitative study.' *Dementia 12*, 4, 410–424.

Kaiser, S. and Panegyres, P.K.(2007) 'The psychosocial impact of young onset dementia on spouses.' *American Journal of Alzheimer's Disease and Other Dementias 21*, 6, 398–402.

Kipps, C.M., Mioshi, E. and Hodges, J.R. (2009) 'Emotion, social functioning and activities of daily living in frontotemporal dementia.' *Neurocase 15*, 3, 182–189.

Koch, T. and Iliffe, S. (2011) 'Dementia diagnosis and management: A narrative review of changing practice.' *British Journal of General Practice 61*, 589, 513–525.

La Fontaine, J. and Oyebode, J.R. (2014) 'Family Relationships and Dementia: A Synthesis of Qualitative Research Including the Person with Dementia in Service Development and Evaluation.' In M. Downs and B. Bowers (eds) *Excellence in Dementia Care: Research into Practice (2nd edition)*. Berkshire: Open University Press.

Litherland, R. and Capstick, A. (2014) 'Involving People with Dementia in Service Development and Evaluation.' In M. Downs and B. Bowers (eds) *Excellence in Dementia Care: Research into Practice (2nd edition)*. Berkshire: Open University Press.

Lockeridge, S. and Simpson, J. (2012) 'The experience of caring for a partner with young onset dementia: How younger carers cope.' *Dementia 12*, 5, 635–651.

Mayrhofer, A., Mathie, E., McKeown, J., Bunn, F. and Goodman, C. (2017) 'Age-appropriate services for people diagnosed with young onset dementia (YOD): A systematic review.' *Aging and Mental Health*. Accessed on 16/10/17 at www.tandfonline.com/doi/full/10.1080/13607863.2017.1334038

Mioshi, E., Foxe, D., Leslie, F., Savage, S. *et al.* (2013) 'The impact of dementia severity on caregiver burden in frontotemporal dementia and Alzheimer's disease.' *Alzheimer Disease Associated Disorders 27,* 1, 68–73.

Nay, R., Bauer, M., Fetherstonhaugh, D., Moyle, W., Tarzia, L. and McAuliffe, L. (2015) 'Social participation and family carers of people living with dementia in Australia.' *Health and Social Care in the Community 23,* 5, 550–558.

Nicolaou, P., Egan, S.J., Gasson, N. and Kane, R. (2010) 'Identifying needs, burden and distress of carers of people with frontotemporal dementia compared to Alzheimer's disease.' *Dementia 9,* 2, 215–235.

Oyebode, J.R., Bradley, P. and Allen, J.L. (2013) 'Relatives experiences of frontal-variant frontotemporal dementia.' *Qualitative Health Research 23,* 2, 156–166.

Peel, E. and Harding, R. (2013) '"It's a huge maze, the system, it's a terrible maze". Dementia carers' construction of navigating health and social care services.' *Dementia 0,* 0, 1–20.

Riedijk, S.R., De Vugt, M.E., Duivenvoorden, H.J., Niermeijer, M.F. *et al.* (2006) 'Caregiver burden, health-related quality of life and coping in dementia caregivers: A comparison of frontotemporal dementia and Alzheimer's disease.' *Dementia and Geriatric Cognitive Disorders 22,* 405–412.

Svanberg, E., Stott, J. and Spector, A. (2010) '"Just helping": Children living with a parent with young onset dementia.' *Aging and Mental Health 14,* 6, 740–751.

Van Vliet, D., de Vugt, M.E., Bakker, C., Koopmans. C.M. and Verhey, F.R.J. (2010) 'Impact of early onset dementia on caregivers: A review.' *International Journal of Geriatric Psychiatry 25.* 1091–1100.

Werner, P., Stein-Shvachman, I. and Korczyn, A.D. (2009) 'Early onset dementia: Clinical and social aspects.' *International Psychogeriatrics 21,* 4, 631–636.

CHAPTER 5

The Impact of Young Onset Dementia on Family Relationships

Rationale

This chapter will consider the impact of a diagnosis of young onset dementia on the family, exploring the spousal and parent–child relationships. Understanding how to best support families as well as the person with dementia is important, as families can experience a sense of loss or grief after a diagnosis. The diagnosis can also lead to an unexpected future which had not been planned for; furthermore, the person with dementia and family members can experience physical and mental health issues which impact on their wellbeing and quality of life. Learning points will therefore examine ways to offer appropriate support and information to enable families to plan and prepare for living with a diagnosis of dementia.

Learning objectives

The learning objectives for this chapter are to:

- Understand what impact a diagnosis of dementia can have on the whole family.

- Identify ways to support and provide information to help families prepare for living with a diagnosis of dementia.

- Understand the value of working and speaking with the family about what they would like to know and how to best support them.

Introduction

Following a diagnosis of dementia, health and social care practitioners may find that they are not only dealing with the person with the dementia but also the wider family and their social situation, therefore an awareness of these issues and an understanding of how to support families is essential.

Young onset dementia is often considered in terms of its impact on the 'life phase' (van Vliet *et al.* 2010a) and how it can change expected future plans. The diagnosis of dementia can impact on a person's social and personal relationships, as has been discussed through changes in employment, adopting caring roles, loss of independence and changes to marital and parental relationships (Harris and Keady 2004; van Vliet *et al.* 2010a; Green and Kleissen 2013; Wawrziczny *et al.* 2016). This can result in people experiencing psychological and emotional difficulties, feeling stigmatised by the dementia and becoming increasingly socially isolated from their community, friends and family. This is something that can be experienced by the person with the diagnosis and the immediate family members (Harris and Keady 2004; Pipon-Young *et al.* 2012; Clemerson, Walsh and Isaac 2014). Consideration may also be required for the type of dementia which an individual has, as a person with a diagnosis of Alzheimer's disease will have a different experience to someone with a diagnosis of frontotemporal dementia.

This chapter will explore the emotional and relational impacts for the family, with consideration given to how the parent–child relationship can change, as well as considering the coping strategies family members can adopt. This discussion is drawn from personal stories and research which explore the impact of young onset dementia on spousal and parent–child relationships and concludes with learning points which examine ways to support families and improve communication, and reflect on what information families need to plan and prepare for living with a diagnosis.

Changing roles, life course perspective

What is often characterised by young onset dementia is the life-course perspective, where there is a change in a person's expected life path, i.e. what is planned for and expected to happen. This can have a significant impact for not only the person diagnosed with a dementia but also their family and friends (van Vliet *et al.*, 2010b), as people negotiate the contradictions between a planned future and one which includes living with a dementia.

The impact of young onset dementia on the family can be profound, with some families reporting higher levels of stress and conflict within the family unit after a diagnosis of dementia (Barca *et al.* 2014). Changing roles within the family can be one of the key drivers behind this stress. This can be experienced by all members of the family, for example, children may suddenly find they are taking on a caring role for their parent, parents can be caring for adult children and spouses have to negotiate changing marital and sexual relationships (Wawrziczny *et al.* 2016). Alongside this, families may find they have to deal with financial pressures as parents' work roles alter (e.g. going part-time, taking early retirement), while children may even find they are seeking employment to support the household (Allen, Oyebode and Allen 2009; Barca *et al.* 2014).

One area where there has been much research is in understanding the impact of a diagnosis on children within the family, particularly those who take on a caring role. However, little is known about the number of children this may affect (National Children's Bureau 2016). There needs to be greater awareness of the needs of young people and how to adequately provide support which is tailored to their age and requirements. What is known, however, is that the impact of a parent's diagnosis of dementia on children is complex and affects all aspects of their lives and relationships.

A study by Allen *et al.* (2009) of young people, aged 13–23, with a father with young onset dementia, identified that children can experience stress and other psychological factors related to the redefining of parental relationships and of the unexpected nature of the diagnosis. According to Allen and colleagues, children are managing the changing progression of the disease, seeing parents' behaviour, physical abilities and memory change. This may lead to the breakdown of relationships, feelings of guilt and a collapse of the family unit, as Anna explains:

> When our son came back from university after six months [Bill] his father showed no signs of recognition at all. He (son) is very reluctant to come home now, as I don't think he feels he fits in. In the event of course, he feels guilty that he isn't here and helping us. They (sons) know as well as I do there is only horribleness to come. (Anna, husband diagnosed in 2012; quoted in Hayo (2016, p.169))

Furthermore, these changes in family dynamics can lead to a change in the family hierarchy (Westman 2000). Children may experience the changing role of their parents within the household and find that they are taking on more of a parental role (see Case study 5.1).

CASE STUDY 5.1

Beth's father was diagnosed with vascular dementia ten years after first showing signs of dementia. Beth explains that even though the family was not aware that her father was experiencing symptoms of dementia, they were aware that he was not well. This was initially thought to be the result of a change in his circumstances as her father had recently retired. However, the symptoms continued to develop and what was thought to be a phase of adjustment eventually resulted in a diagnosis of dementia. Beth's father's dementia was exhibited through a change in personality and through a lack of motivation and interest in activities, particularly previously enjoyed hobbies, such as gardening. This extended into a loss of interest in his own personal care as he stopped washing himself or changing his clothes and bed sheets. Beth, aged 12 when her father first showed signs of dementia, explains how she would take over these tasks, helping to change the bed sheets, persuading her father to wash and cut his hair and helping to make drinks. Beth and her family also had to make a difficult decision about when her father should stop driving, a process that required sensitivity and a recognition that this was a loss of a part of his status as an adult and of his independence. Beth did not see this as taking over the care of her father but rather this was a way to compensate for the changes in his abilities and judgement.

As in Beth's example, children can take on responsibilities within the household. Some of these responsibilities are associated with offering safety and security, not just to protect the parent with dementia, but to support the parent without the diagnosis (Allen *et al.* 2009). These changes in roles may not always be recognised by the children as part of the caring process, as Beth discussed, this care was part of coping and adapting to the changes her father experienced and she explains that it was 'a way of getting on with everyday life'.

Children may also feel the need to stay at home rather than move out in order to provide care for both parents, offering protection from others and helping to keep the sense of normality within the household (Allen *et al.* 2009; Millenaar *et al.* 2014; Hutchinson *et al.* 2016). This may also result in young people feeling the need to drop out of school and change future plans to support their families, for example choosing to go into work rather than go to university, therefore helping support the family finances (Allen *et al.* 2009), essentially putting 'their lives on hold' in order to care for their family (Sikes and Hall 2017, p.8).

The degree to which the changing role of the child within the household is influenced may be due to the level of change seen with their parents. Significant changes made to work and social life can be reflected in the level of support children offer their parents. The level of support offered by outside agencies, be this formally through health and social care services, or informally through the wider family and community, can also have an influence on the changing nature of the roles and added responsibility taken on by children (Allen *et al.* 2009), with greater support lessening the burden on the family.

The relationships between the child and parent can be tested following a diagnosis of dementia. As care and support is focused on the parent with dementia, both parents can become 'emotionally unavailable' to the child, challenging their relationships and potentially drawing out feelings of resentfulness and no longer belonging in the family (Allen *et al.* 2009). The loss of a close relationship is explained by Jane, who talks of her daughter's distress at the loss of a close father/daughter relationship:

> Our eldest daughter in particular expressed her upset at his detachment, especially as they had been close before and said he was not behaving as she would like her father to be. (Jane, husband symptomatic from 2010; quoted in Hayo (2016, p.139))

However, children can adapt, through a process of grieving for the old relationship and separating from the parent emotionally, to being able to take on a new adult role. This in turn leads to the formation of a new relationship status between the parent and child (Svanberg, Stott and Spector 2010). In practice though, this requires support and time. There are ways in which families can be supported to negotiate these changing relationships, for example, by working with the families to share their experiences, and finding ways to support their emotional resilience and independence. Health and social care practitioners can consider asking how family members are dealing with the diagnosis, in particular children, and think about the support they may need if taking on a caring role (Svanberg *et al.* 2010) or identifying suitable role models or support networks.

As well as looking at children within the family, the role of the partner or spouse must also be considered. The caring role will predominantly be taken on by a partner or spouse and this can be challenging to manage, with physical, cognitive and psychological changes occurring in their cared-for person. There may also be difficult decisions to be made in terms of disclosing the diagnosis. In interviews with spouses, Ducharme and colleagues (2013) found that often spouses did not want to tell other people, including friends and other family members, about the diagnosis. They felt there was a prevalent stigma associated with dementia which could lead to misunderstandings about the condition, with participants in this study reporting having been given false advice or being blamed for the illness. This stigma was a source of growing isolation and often it was only at a point of crisis that the diagnosis had to be disclosed. Finding a way to cope with the changes of dementia and to be open about these is one way of encouraging families to engage with the outside world, and so reducing the isolation they can experience (Wawrziczny *et al.* 2016).

In Ducharme *et al*'s (2013) study, spouses reported feeling a sense of grief at the loss of their married life and change in circumstances and roles. Support could be provided to spousal/partner carers to maintain relationships and to come to terms with the changes. However, it should be acknowledged that following the diagnosis of dementia, there may be a change to the relationship or even marital breakdown. Mood swings, changes to, or inappropriate behaviour can result in a change in the way a partner is seen. This can lead a partner or spouse not recognising their partner as the person they fell in love with. Sue explains how changes in her husband led to feelings of alienation from him:

> I think one of the saddest aspects was that before you get the diagnosis you already feel alienated from the person. I started to feel not interested in this person or his behaviours. (Sue, husband symptomatic from 2011; quoted in Hayo (2016, p.164))

The changes in roles could be due to the loss of engaging in everyday activities formerly enjoyed as a couple or family, such as going out. Encouraging open and honest communication is one way of managing these changing relationships; including relationship discussions within a care plan can be one way of providing support to maintain these relationships (Ducharme *et al.* 2013; Wawrziczny *et al.* 2016).

Furthermore, couples may have to negotiate their sexual relationships, something which can impact on their sense of self-worth and quality of life. Changes in sexual relationships can be complex, whether it be a loss of sexual activity or an increase. If, and what type of, changes may occur for a person with dementia in relation to their sexual needs will depend on the type of dementia and what parts of the brain have been affected. A person can become more aggressive in their sexual demands or become less inhibited in their behaviour. This can be distressing and embarrassing for a partner, who may need to seek professional advice. Conversely, a partner who loses their sexual desires can leave the other person feeling frustrated, unloved and unwanted. Everyone's experiences will differ but changing sexual relations is a normal part of any relationship, whether a person has dementia or not. Health and social care practitioners should be aware that these changes can occur and be willing to raise these often sensitive issues, offering suggestions to cope with the changes, for example: talking to a close family or friend; seeking relationship advice; and understanding different ways of expressing intimacy. Being open about these issues is the first step to being able to support couples experiencing issues with their sexual relationships properly (Alzheimer's Society 2015).

Emotional stress and wellbeing

The diagnosis of dementia can result in depression, stress, carer burden and poor health (NICE 2006; Jefferies and Agrawal 2009; Bakker *et al.* 2010; van Vliet *et al.* 2010b). One possible reason for this is having to deal with changes in the person with dementia's behaviour, especially when negative or aggressive behaviour develops. Sue speaks of her husband's 'Victorian' behaviour and its impact on her relationship:

> Initially I just thought he was getting more like his dad, he was very Victorian and I thought that this was the route we were going down. I thought I would soon sort this out, but no. He's not the person I married. (Sue, husband symptomatic from 2011; quoted in Hayo (2016, p.135))

Stress may also result from a loss of activities, loss of friendships and financial pressures (Gelman and Greer 2011). This stress can manifest in many ways and may be seen as a physical and psychological impact, through: loss of sleep; worry; emotional sense of loss; ceasing to express or hiding emotions; loss of happiness; isolation; and resentment (Allen *et al.* 2009).

As with research on changing roles, research on emotional impact has focused on children. It has been identified that a lack of support and recognition for changes in roles, and the stigma related to dementia, can have a negative impact on emotional wellbeing (Hutchinson *et al.* 2015). Hutchinson *et al.* (2015) found the stigma of dementia could result in loss of friendships and feelings of burden by the lack of understanding and knowledge in the wider society about dementia. Not only can the stigma of dementia be shown by those outside of the family unit, but also within, resulting in feelings of shame or confusion about the diagnosis (Allen *et al.* 2009; Hutchinson *et al.* 2016), resulting in children distancing themselves from family and friends as they withdraw, not wanting to talk about dementia.

One way in which services can support wellbeing within families is to identify ways to recognise the role children play within the family, by providing advice and finding ways to enable children to speak about their concerns. This can mitigate any feelings of neglect that children may feel from the wider family and services.

Coping strategies

Coping strategies have been identified as a key way that families manage a diagnosis of dementia. The focus of research in this area is often on how children cope and what strategies they put in place to manage a parent with dementia's changing behaviours, dealing with taking on a caring role and how they maintain their mental wellbeing. The diagnosis of dementia can have a negative impact on the family; however, evidence also suggests that families do cope and find ways to adapt if they are given the appropriate support, from services and other family members (Cabote, Bramble and McCann 2015; Deist and Greeff 2015), and given information about dementia (Baptista *et al.* 2016).

An early study by Allen *et al.* (2009) identified a number of coping strategies used by young people whose father had a diagnosis of young onset dementia. These young people spoke of doing everyday activities with their father, such as having a meal or going shopping, as a way for them to feel as though life was 'normal'. Keeping active and busy with school or work was also discussed as a way of distracting themselves from the situation at home. However, these strategies were also countered with less constructive strategies, such as consuming alcohol, smoking, detaching themselves from the situation and not dealing with the issues. Perhaps the main coping strategy which the young people in Allen and colleagues' study reported was the idea of taking 'one day at a time' (p.471), that dealing with an unknown and often fearful future was too difficult and could be overwhelming, therefore dealing with the present was a strong coping mechanism.

A more recent study, by Millenaar *et al.* (2014), supports and extends the range of coping strategies employed by young people. A diagnosis of dementia can have both a positive and negative impact: it can lead to stronger family relationships, but it can also bring stress and conflict. As such, children develop different coping strategies. Alongside those discussed, children can choose to avoid the diagnosis by not seeking out information, or avoiding potentially confrontational situations. This is exemplified through avoiding talk of 'correcting' a parent's behaviour (Millenaar *et al.* 2014) or hiding their feelings about the impact of the dementia. Another coping mechanism is adapting behaviours to support and preserve the abilities of the cared for person, their independence and personal interests (Le Galès and Bungener 2016). Health and social care practitioners need to understand that the individuals within each family unit will respond to the diagnosis in their own ways. The challenge faced is therefore in recognising this and finding the right support which will work for each family. In this way, health and social care practitioners can support the more positive coping strategies for managing and living with a diagnosis of dementia.

One way of providing this support is to ensure families have time to talk, to a family member or support worker, about the issues they face. Furthermore, finding a role model or mentor for a child to talk with can encourage children to share their experiences, concerns and feelings, and is a way to support their development and learning (Denny *et al.* 2012). Gelman and Greer (2011) found a role model helped children with everyday activities and developmental activities, such as learning to drive, and, importantly, feeling less isolated. Children often want to talk to someone with knowledge of young onset dementia and this can be a way to help build trust and relationships with service providers (Millenaar *et al.* 2014). A role model or mentor might not always be appropriate for children, so encouraging them to take part in school clubs and to engage with their peers can also be a positive way of ensuring children do not become isolated and are still engaged outside of the household (Gelman and Greer 2011). Finding a safe space for children to share their experiences and to talk about what is happening to them and their family can be a way of coming to terms with the dementia, even if these stories are painful and difficult to share (Hall and Sikes 2014). However, the timing of this should be carefully considered as not all children want or should be told about the diagnosis straight away. This is something that should be done in consultation with the parents (Millenaar *et al.* 2014).

It is not only young children that develop coping strategies. Older children and adults also develop ways in which they can deal with the emotional and physical demands of a diagnosis. These reflect those adopted by younger children, as can be exemplified in research by Lockeridge and Simpson (2013) who interviewed six spousal carers about their coping strategies. Denial of the diagnosis was a commonly adopted strategy, through avoidance of the situation, and as such provided a layer of self-protection (Clare 2003). This is explained by Angela, who feels the strain this brings.

Now I've got the diagnosis it gives a reason to some of the behaviours. I don't get irritated by his behaviour; I just ignore it and avoid getting into a situation where it could become annoying. Sometimes I think it's such a long period without having anybody to talk to about this, no one to rely on and always working around the other person. Always working around their needs and it gets very wearing. (Angela, husband diagnosed 2012; quoted in Hayo (2016, p.165))

Further coping strategies can see family members trying to compensate for their partner: this may be by rationalising their behaviour or by taking on activities which they find difficult or can no longer manage (as was discussed in Beth's case study – she helped her father with washing and looking after the garden). Even seemingly simple activities such as making a cup of tea are actually quite complex and require a lot of knowledge, memory and processing to complete. Tasks such as this may be taken over by the family members (Lockeridge and Simpson 2013). While this may seem to be a form of protection for the person with dementia, the theory of 'use it or lose it' may also be applicable here. Health and social care practitioners can encourage family members to work with their cared-for person to continue to do activities for as long as possible, working with them to do the task, rather than taking this over entirely. This may provide opportunities for working with an occupational therapist to understand how to provide this support and how to adapt the household to encourage greater engagement in daily activities.

Family members can feel a lack of control about how they provide care. One way of coping with this is to turn to other family members for advice and support. Knowledge of and being able to signpost family members to support groups, carer networks and navigating care pathways can be a valuable way of supporting them. Peer support can provide reassurances, learning and information about dementia and is a key coping strategy for most family members. Starting points for access to support groups include the local Alzheimer's Society, carer organisations, Dementia UK and Age UK.

Information

Providing information about young onset dementia can be one way to support families; however, when and how to deliver this information must be carefully considered. Families will respond differently, some may want to find out all they can in order to be knowledgeable and to understand how to respond to the diagnosis, while others may be fearful of knowing too much. While knowledge may enable people to understand more about young onset dementia, it may also bring greater levels of stress as people will find out how the dementia could progress. There is a difficult balance to be found in providing enough information but not so much that it may overwhelm the family. Dealing with this on a case-by-case basis is necessary to understand how much the family want to know and what will be suitable to ensure that they are able to manage the dementia appropriately (Allen *et al.* 2009). An honest and open approach to discussing young onset dementia with families is best (Denny *et al.* 2012).

Information can help in a number of ways: not only can families have a greater understanding of what dementia is and how to support the person they are caring for, but also it is a way to help them to feel valued and to plan for the future, such as putting in place power of attorney, a will and care plans. Greater communication and information about dementia and the services which could be accessed will mean a family are more able to access activities, arrange respite time, have tailored support and have a multi-professional team working with the family to ensure the best care is provided for all its members (Ducharme *et al.* 2014). Beth's experience with her father's dementia exemplifies how a lack of support and information can lead to a crisis point (see Case study 5.2).

CASE STUDY 5.2

Beth's father was seen regularly by his GP. The family acknowledges that 'life was not right at home' but felt reassured that the GP would identify any serious health concerns. Beth describes her father as a proud man, who was always self-sufficient. She accepts that, because of this, her father may have decided not to tell his family about a diagnosis. She reports that her father had been visited by a consultant in the months before a formal diagnosis was made. At this consultation, the family were not involved or informed of any issues. Ten years after the first symptoms were noticed by the family, Beth's father had a stroke which led to his hospitalisation and a formal diagnosis of dementia. The family was informed by the consultant that he had known for several months prior about the diagnosis, but because her father did not want any help, no support could be offered until a crisis occurred. This lack of involvement with the family meant that support from meals on wheels, social services and the consultant were not available. Beth's family would have welcomed support but this was not made available because the decision rested with her father alone and no inclusion of the family was made in earlier consultations or in considering the impact on them as a family. Beth feels health professionals would benefit from speaking with families as they provide a different perspective and experience, offering personal knowledge and understanding of the individual. Beth advocates for a 'team' approach when providing care for someone with dementia; where the person, their family, and health and social care professionals work together to ensure that everyone is supported appropriately.

Conclusion

There are many ways in which a diagnosis of young onset dementia can impact on the family. Families have to negotiate changes in all aspects of their lives. What research shows is the loyalty of the family to maintain and support each other and to find ways of coping and managing with a diagnosis of young onset dementia. The diagnosis of dementia can feel like a process of grief and loss for many (Sikes and Hall 2017) and stigma of young onset dementia is still a concern. The individual way people respond to a diagnosis of dementia is important to recognise for health and social care providers, who should consider how to respond to them on an individual basis, but also consider offering a 'family-centred approach' to the provision of services (Chemali, Withall and Daffner 2010; Ducharme *et al.* 2014; Hutchinson *et al.* 2016). This means looking at the family unit as a whole rather than just the person with the diagnosis and considering all aspects of their health and care needs, be those mental health issues or financial and legal concerns. It is important that holistic and inter-professional support is offered (Hutchinson *et al.* 2016). The Prime Minister's challenge on dementia 2020 (DH 2015) identifies the need for personalised care that is responsive to the needs of the person with dementia and the family, focusing on the need for greater 'choice, control and flexibility' (p.27) over the support which families receive. And it is by responding to the care needs in this way that health and social care practitioners can support families to minimise the impact on their relationships and to support them to navigate the complex care pathways.

KEY POINTS

1. Consider ways to keep families connected to their friends, family and communities.

2. It is important to have an open discussion with families following a diagnosis of dementia and to keep that dialogue ongoing to support families as their needs may change. Families should be included in the care and support plans to ensure these are working for the best interests of the person with dementia and the family. However, be mindful that not everyone wants to talk about the diagnosis of dementia and that some families may delay telling younger children.

3. Consider the whole family unit, not just the main carer and the person with dementia, by asking 'How is dementia affecting others in the household?'

4. Think about the support that can be offered to children within the family, such as a mentor or access to school activities, which can support them to engage with peers and to have interests outside of the family.

5. Support is both health and social focused; therefore, working collaboratively will give the best tailored support to families. Provide information and signposting to support services.

References

Allen, J., Oyebode, J.R. and Allen J. (2009) 'Having a father with young onset dementia. The impact on well-being of young people.' *Dementia 8*, 4, 455–480.

Alzheimer's Society (2015) *Sex and intimate relationships. Factsheet 514LP.* London: Alzheimer's Society.

Bakker, C., de Vugt, M.E., Vernooij-Dassen, M., van Vliet, D., Verhey, F.R.J. and Koopmans, R.T. (2010) 'Needs in early onset dementia: A qualitative case from the NeedYD study.' *American Journal of Alzheimer's Disease and Other Dementias 25*, 8, 634–640.

Baptista, M.A.T., Santos, R.L., Kimura, N., Lacerda, I.B. *et al.* (2016) 'Quality of life in young onset dementia: An updated systematic review.' *Trends in Psychiatry and Psychotherapy 38*, 1, 6–13.

Barca, M.L., Thorsen, K., Engedal, K., Haugen, P.K. and Johannessen, A. (2014) 'Nobody asked me how I felt: Experiences of adult children of persons with young-onset dementia.' *International Psychogeriatrics 26*, 12, 1935–1944.

Cabote, C.J., Bramble, M. and McCann, D. (2015) 'Family caregivers' experiences of caring for a relative with younger onset dementia: A qualitative systematic review.' *Journal of Family Nursing 21*, 3, 443–468.

Chemali, Z., Withall, A. and Daffner, K.R. (2010) 'The plight of caring for young patients with frontotemporal dementia.' *American Journal of Alzheimer's Disease and Other Dementias 25*, 2, 109–115.

Clare, L. (2003) 'Managing threats to self: Awareness in early stage Alzheimer's disease.' *Social Science and Medicine 57*, 6, 1017–1029.

Clemerson, G., Walsh, S. and Isaac, C. (2014) 'Towards living well with young onset dementia: An exploration of coping from the perspective of those diagnosed.' *Dementia 13*, 4, 451–466.

Deist, M. and Greeff, A.P. (2015) 'Living with a parent with dementia: A family resilience study.' *Dementia 0*, 0, 1–16.

Denny, S.S., Morhardt, D., Gaul, J.C., Lester, L., Andersen, G., Higgins, P.J. and Nee, L. (2012) 'Caring for children of parents with frontotemporal degeneration: A report of the AFTD Task Force on families with children.' *American Journal of Alzheimer's Disease and Other Dementias 27*, 8, 568–578.

Department of Health (2015) Prime Minister's Challenge on Dementia 2020. London: DH.

Ducharme, F., Kergoat, M-J., Antoine, P., Pasquier, F. and Coulombe, R. (2013) 'The unique experience of spouses in early-onset dementia.' *American Journal of Alzheimer's Disease and Other Dementias 28*, 6, 634–641.

Ducharme, F., Kergoat, M-J., Coulombe, R., Lvesque, L., Antoine, P. and Pasquier, F. (2014) 'Unmet support needs of early-onset dementia family caregivers: A mixed-design study.' *BMC Nursing 13*, 49, 1–10.

Gelman, C.R. and Greer, C. (2011) 'Young children in early-onset Alzheimer's disease families: Research gaps and emerging service needs.' *American Journal of Alzheimer's Disease and Other Dementias 26*, 1, 29–35.

Green, T. and Kleissen, T. (2013) 'Early onset dementia: A narrative review of the literature.' *Indian Journal of Gerontology 27*, 1, 1–28.

Hall, M. and Sikes, P. (2014) '"It would be easier if she'd died": Young people with parents with dementia articulating inadmissible stories.' *Qualitative Health Research 27*, 8, 1203–1214.

Harris, P. and Keady, J. (2004) 'Living with early onset dementia: Exploring the experience and developing evidence-based guidelines for practice.' *Alzheimer's Care Quarterly 5*, 2, 111–122.

Hayo, H. (2016) 'How and why does social connectedness change in families living with the effects of behavioural variant frontotemporal dementia?' Doctor of Professional Practice. University of Northampton, Northampton.

Hutchinson, K., Roberts, C., Daly, M., Bulsara, C. and Kurrle, S. (2015) 'Empowerment of young people who have a parent living with dementia: A social model perspective.' *International Psychogeriatrics 28*, 4, 657–668.

Hutchinson, K., Roberts, C., Kurrle, S. and Daly, M. (2016) 'The emotional well-being of young people having a parent with younger onset dementia.' *Dementia 15*, 4, 609–628.

Jefferies, K. and Agrawal, N. (2009) 'Early-onset dementia.' *Advances in Psychiatric Treatment 15*, 380–388.

Le Galès, C. and Bungener, M. (2016) 'The family accompaniment of persons with dementia seen through the lens of the capability approach.' *Dementia 0*, 0, 1–25.

Lockeridge, S. and Simpson, J. (2013) 'The experience of caring for a partner with young onset dementia: How younger carers cope.' *Dementia 12*, 5, 635–651.

Millenaar, J.K., van Vliet, D., Bakker, C., Vernooij-Dassen, M.J.F.J., Koopmans, R.T.C.M., Verhey, F.R.J. and de Vugt, M.E. (2014) 'The experiences and needs of children living with a parent with young onset dementia: Results from the NeedYD study.' *International Psychogeriatrics 26*, 12, 2001–2010.

National Children's Bureau (2016) Young people caring for adults with dementia in England. Report on NCB's survey findings and internet research. London: National Children's Bureau.

National Institute for Health and Care Excellence (NICE) (2006) *Dementia: Supporting people with dementia and their carers in health and social care.* NICE Clinical Guideline 42. London: NICE.

Pipon-Young, F.E., Lee, K.M., Jones, F. and Guss, R. (2012) '"I'm not all gone, I can still speak": The experiences of younger people with dementia. An action research study.' *Dementia 11*, 5, 597–616.

Sikes, P. and Hall, M. (2017) '"Every time I see him he's the worst he's ever been and the best he'll ever be": Grief and sadness in children and young people who have a parent with dementia.' *Mortality 22*, 4, 324–338.

Svanberg, E., Stott, J. and Spector, A. (2010) '"Just Helping": Children living with a parent with young onset dementia.' *Aging and Mental Health 14*, 6, 740–751.

van Vliet, D., Bakker, C., Koopmans, R., Vernooij-Dassen, M., Verhey, F. and de Vugt, M.D. (2010a) 'Research protocol for the NeedYD-study (Needs in Young onset Dementia): A prospective cohort study on the needs and course of early onset dementia.' *BMC Geriatrics 10*, 1, 13–21.

van Vliet, D., de Vugt, M.D., Bakker, C., Koopmans, R. and Verhey, F. (2010b) 'Impact of early onset dementia on caregivers: A review.' *International Journal of Geriatric Psychiatry 25*, 1091–1100.

Wawrziczny, E., Antoine, P., Ducharme, F., Kergoat, M-J. and Pasquier, F. (2016) 'Couples' experiences with early-onset dementia: An interpretative phenomenological analysis of dyadic dynamics.' *Dementia 15*, 5, 1082–1099.

Westman, A. (2000) 'The Problem of Parental Personality.' In P. Reder, M. McClure and A. Jolley (eds) *Family Matters: Interfaces between Child and Adult Mental Health*. London: Routledge.

CHAPTER 6

Lonely in a Social World

Maintaining Social Connections in Young Onset Dementia

Rationale

The aim of this chapter is to outline how receiving a diagnosis of dementia, as a person of working age, can significantly impact on both the person with dementia and their family, in terms of both diminishing social connections and increased feelings of loneliness. It will indicate how health and social care practitioners can support people living with young onset dementia and their families to continue to participate in meaningful social activities in order to help them to retain their social connectivity and maintain their psychosocial wellbeing.

To stay mentally and physically well after diagnosis, and to reduce the effects of increased loneliness and social isolation, it is important that the person with dementia and their family stay socially connected. Practitioners can help by spending time getting to know the person and their family, establishing what type of social support is needed, and signposting them to suitable community-based groups where appropriate. This should take account of the person's/carer's needs, interests, hobbies, skills and abilities, knowledge and experience. The family may be offered a referral to a specialist support group in the locality if one is available. The benefits of attending such groups include peer support, age appropriate information, and a safe and comfortable environment.

Learning objectives

The learning objectives for this chapter are to:

- Explore the impact on relationships and social connections for the younger person with dementia and their family.

- Identify how specialist support groups can be beneficial in reducing the effects of social isolation and loneliness in people with a diagnosis and their families.

- Consider how health and social care practitioners can support the individual and their family in accessing appropriate specialist community-based social support groups.

Introduction

When a person is diagnosed with a dementia, the person themselves, as well as their family and friends, can experience strong feelings associated with multiple losses. For the person with a diagnosis, as the memory fades, these losses can be profound. Initially, they might include loss of employment, loss of access to a vehicle, and reduced ability to engage in meaningful hobbies and activities, leading to diminished autonomy and independence. In addition, the person may experience intense feelings of grief as relationships are altered and lost, memories grow dim, and the individual's sense of self becomes significantly altered. Furthermore, families can also experience bereavement when faced with a future of caring for their loved one. This grief reaction can be attributed to losses associated with their relationship including: loss of intimacy, companionship and support, and conversation; changes to their shared lifestyle together (e.g. hobbies and activities and plans for the future) and the lifestyle modifications they will need to make to accommodate their ever-changing caring role.

For people living with a young onset dementia, the physical, psychological, and social impact of the disease process on both the individual with a diagnosis and their family is enormous. As the individual and family members begin to notice and experience progressive cognitive decline and other impacts of the diagnosis, both they and their family can begin to feel socially isolated, and increasingly alone. This may be due to waning self-confidence, over-protectiveness, and embarrassment, or even because former friends and colleagues begin to avoid contact. Barbara describes how long term friends of her husband, Roger, and herself immediately stopped coming to visit them as soon as he was diagnosed with dementia (see Case study 6.1).

CASE STUDY 6.1

Barbara: Well, we didn't have any social life, you see.

Interviewer: And did you find that hard?

Barbara: I did, we had this friend that lived locally and he was the boy next door, Eddie was the boy next door and that's who we was at Tenerife, when we went to Tenerife with, so I've known, we've known each other all our lives and on a Friday we always went up to Eddie's to play cribbage you see, always went to play cribbage, Friday nights. Well, Eddie had noticed, and Enid, and of course I had, that he was getting slower, Roger was getting slower and he wasn't playing the cards that he should have played, but we didn't take any notice, we just sort of let it go. Now, they was what I should say was our closest friends, and when Roger got diagnosed like with the dementia it just all stopped, and I mean you can count on that hand how many times I've seen them since Roger died.

Interviewer: Really?

Barbara: Mmmm. And that's the boy next door, you know, sort of, known all my living life...but it's strange how people react. I can't...

The effects of loneliness and social isolation

The instinctive need for love, intimacy, and social affiliation is inherently part of being human. It is a defining characteristic, which means that most individuals prefer to live in the company of others, or in communities, rather than in isolation (Baumeister *et al.* 2005). Genetically predisposed, the desire to be in close proximity with other people can make individuals feels safe and protected as well as ensuring the survival of the species (Baumeister and Leary 1995; Cacioppo and Patrick 2008).

Choosing to be alone and subjective feelings of loneliness are different experiences. Every individual is equipped with an instinctive disposition to avoid the perceived dangers associated with being alone and feeling vulnerable. When people are unable to maintain the level of social connection they feel is meaningful for them, they can experience both the physical and psychological sensations associated with social pain. Loneliness is considered in terms of emotional and social isolation, with the two states being closely aligned. Loneliness is usually perceived as a negative emotion, which is painful and uniquely experienced (Masi *et al.* 2011). It is thought to be an 'emotional state' faced by the individual who experiences distance or separation from other people, while simultaneously wanting the company of others. However, feelings of loneliness protect people from social isolation by motivating them to work at building, sustaining or restoring those social bonds which make them feel happy and promote a sense of mental wellbeing (Masi *et al.* 2011).

Increasingly, due to the growing body of evidence connecting it with negative health and wellbeing outcomes, severe or chronic loneliness is being recognised as a public health concern (Kawachi and Berkman 2001; Kok *et al.* 2013). Frequently associated with the loss of a significant relationship or a life event, i.e. divorce, separation, bereavement, or retirement, the subjective feelings associated with loneliness, if sustained, can lead to feelings of anxiety, stress, and depression. In 1985, Cohen and Willis put forward two models that are not mutually exclusive, which explain the interaction between the maintenance of social relationships and positive health outcomes. In the 'Stress-Buffering Model', the perceived availability of positive social support can help an individual to moderate their responses to stressful events. Whereas the 'Main Effects Model' explains how continued participation in the structural aspects of social relationships, such as social networks, can positively affect psychological wellbeing. Remaining socially integrated within a community context can provide members with a sense of belonging, purpose, and security, as well as recognition of self-worth.

According to Huber *et al.* (2011) the maintenance of a person's social health requires them to have 'capacity to fulfil their potential and obligations, the ability to manage their life with some degree of independence despite a medical condition, and the ability to participate in social activities including work' (p.2). However, it is well known that the progressive cognitive changes associated with dementia significantly impact on a person's ability to actively engage in social activities. These can include the cognitive ability to attend and physical ability to actively participate. Communication difficulties can also contribute to reduced self confidence in social interactions and situations. In turn, these significant and progressive alterations to self can impact on the person's social health and wellbeing by interfering with their ability to maintain their independence while carrying out everyday activities, sustain social relationships, and contribute to society.

Most young people diagnosed with dementia are cared for at home, often by their spouse or children (Allen, Oyebode and Allen 2009), and social excursions become increasingly restricted in duration and frequency. As such, living with young onset dementia can be a socially isolating experience for all family members (Lockeridge and Simpson 2013; Clemerson *et al.* 2014).

The partners of people living with dementia also have to adjust their recreational and social activities to be inclusive of the person (Hawkins *et al.* 2013). This is primarily because people living with a diagnosis of young onset dementia felt that the negative way others perceived them threatened their identity. Lockeridge and Simpson (2013) reported that the carers of people living with the condition stated that the stress of caring for their loved one could also have a major impact on their own psychosocial wellbeing. They felt increasingly socially isolated through the fear or embarrassment that living with dementia can bring. However, both people living with the condition and their families felt that some social re-connection was possible by sharing their experiences with people in similar situation (Lockeridge and Simpson 2013;

Clemerson *et al.* 2014) provided that it is appropriate for the right age group or that is tailored to different types of dementia. Frank recalls how he began to re-connect with the social world after caring for his relative assisted by a key practitioner, and Admiral Nurse, who was able to work with him to engage with a local support group for carers in similar circumstances (see Case study 6.2).

CASE STUDY 6.2

Frank, who cared for his late mum, recalls how it impacted on his social life especially whilst in full-time employment and later. Previously he would go out with some of his friends at work to socialise, but over time this gradually changed as he felt he needed to spend more time with mum at home to both support her and also keep her company. Also, Frank revealed that no one at work knew about his commitments at home as this was a personal issue he wanted to keep private and separate from his work life.

Subsequently Frank changed his working patterns so that he could work more at home, as the demands of caring for his mum increased over the years.

Eventually Frank took a career break from work as the mental, physical and emotional pressures of both working and caring for his mum was taking its toll on him. He considered this was the best move for both of them, but he now realises this was a big mistake. Suddenly, he went from a situation of having at least some social interaction at work to absolute isolation, stuck at home with his mum, 24 hours a day, seven days a week, with no outlet. Frank felt imprisoned in his own home as the demands and pressures of caring for his mum continued to increase, and in spite of his efforts with their GP he was not receiving any support from his local health and social services departments.

Frank only began to realise his mistake of taking a career break when he subsequently began to receive some support from a local Admiral Nurse. He recalls the very first meeting when he walked into a room full of strangers (i.e. other family carers), which gave him the confidence to talk about what he was going through and the issues he was having to deal with. He remembers the support he received from these other 'strangers', and the short break away from his mum this meeting provided. It was for Frank a 'eureka moment', being able to socialise with other people in the same position, sharing information, advice and ideas helped him better manage himself, which resulted in both his mood improving and being able to care better for his mum, which had a consequential beneficial impact on life at home.

Therefore, given the premise that for most people to enjoy positive social health, they need to feel socially connected, it seems to be essential that people with young onset dementia and their families are provided with the necessary support and opportunities to engage actively in meaningful social networks and activities. However, there is also a need for communities to move away from attitudes which impact negatively on social participation due to stigmatisation and discrimination, and towards providing a supportive environment where both the person living with dementia and their partners can feel cared for, valued, and socially included if we really want to provide person-centred care for the person living with dementia and their family carer (Kitwood 1997; Brooker 2007). Such positive environments should seek to promote social connection, emphasise normalcy, and offer activities which are meaningful, and focus on the remaining capacities of the young person living with a dementia.

Support interventions for maintaining social health

As previously suggested, evidence indicates that there are many factors which can influence people with dementia and their families participating actively in society. The availability of strong community-based social support and care networks can significantly influence participation in everyday life activities. We know that if people with dementia and their partners engage actively in community activities, it can have a very positive influence on their physical and mental wellbeing, but these need to be available for people with dementia and families to access in the first place. In addition, by providing community-based activities for this societal group, communities learn how to positively care for those in their community who are affected by a diagnosis of dementia. As more organisations and community groups discover how they can be involved in meeting the needs of those with a dementia, they become more knowledgeable and confident in providing instrumental and emotional support, which in turn provides affirming constructive feedback, enabling the person themselves to grow in confidence while building on their retained capacities and capabilities. By expanding their knowledge and understanding of the lived experiences of the person with a dementia and those caring for them, communities can positively adapt and change in various and multiple ways to accommodate their need for social inclusion, including businesses and faith groups becoming dementia friendly.

It can be argued that interventions which encourage individuals with a diagnosis to actively engage in social activities serve as opportunities for them to communicate, interact, and converse with others (Jones, Sung, and Moyle 2015). Such experiences can be pleasurable, empowering, and slow cognitive decline (Kuiper *et al.* 2015). Social activity interventions should be specifically designed to enhance positive experiences such as maintaining positive or meaningful social relationships, instead of being problem oriented. The accessibility of the location and the availability of transport can be both a facilitator and a barrier to enabling active participation of people with a dementia in community-based activities. They should also be tailored primarily to the needs of the person with dementia. Examples of such interventions which have been developed in recent years include the Dutch based Meeting Centre Support Programmes (Dröes *et al.* 2004), the Enriched Opportunities Programme (Brooker *et al.* 2011), The Forget-me-not social support groups for people with young onset dementia and their families (Parkes and Ward 2015), intergenerational programmes (Park 2014), small-scale homelike care environments (Charras 2011; Verbeek *et al.* 2014), and green care farms (de Bruin *et al.* 2009).

The benefits of social support groups for young people with dementia: Implications for practice

The benefit of actively engaging in social support groups, not least in maintaining social connections and reducing loneliness, is clearly applicable to all ages of people diagnosed with a dementia and their families (Cohen-Mansfield, Dakheel-Ali and Marx 2009; O'Rourke *et al.* 2015). Beattie *et al.* (2004) acknowledge that support for people living with young onset dementia needs to be specifically designed to fit their needs, providing practical information and training and education for families where appropriate, as well as social support, as well as connecting them to others in a similar situation. In a study by Johannessen and Moller (2011), most participants felt lonely and had lost their sense of social cohesion following diagnosis; however, the findings also highlighted that the deepened social contact enjoyed by members who actively engage in a social support group has the potential to improve their quality of life significantly, as illustrated by Frank in the case study above. It would therefore seem to be essential that groups which can provide active and meaningful social support to people with young onset dementia and their families should be established where a clear need has been identified and sufficient numbers would justify their existence. An example of such a social support group that was established in Northamptonshire in the UK in July 2013 is the Forget-me-nots Group for People with Young Onset Dementia and their families (Parkes and Ward 2015) (see Box 6.1).

Box 6.1: Example of how the Forget-me-nots Group was designed, developed, and implemented.

The Forget-me-nots Group is a joint initiative between the local Alzheimer's Society Group and University Dementia Research Network. Having consulted with young people with dementia and their carers, it appeared there was limited specialist social support available for this unique population group in the county. Carers and people with dementia responding to the consultation made the following recommendations for future services to support their needs:

- Support with existing social networks post diagnosis

- Support to develop new social networks with those going through a similar experience

---

- Need for tailored support for their age group

- Attend social activities in a safe environment.

People appeared to be willing to travel between five and 20 miles to access a specific young onset dementia (YOD) social support group if one was started locally, and most wanted to attend a group for two hours on a monthly basis in a suitable community-based location, i.e. café, restaurant, etc.

Following this consultation, the project steering committee planned and organised the launch of the Forget-me-nots Group. The group meets from 5–7pm on the last Tuesday of each month. Initially, the group chose to meet in a single community venue; however, as the group has developed, they have taken greater ownership over venues and activities. There are now a wider range of venues visited, with a greater county-wide reach, and activities have included: a barge trip; family Christmas meal; Easter picnic in the park; and an annual afternoon tea. However, the group has favoured an evening meal in a local pub as a regular activity. The group has been supported with matched funding from the Higher Education Institution (HEI) in terms of academic staff time, but in addition, each meeting is supported by volunteers.

The group decided on their name and put forward ideas for a group logo, taking the forget-me-not flower used by the Alzheimer's Society as their inspiration. The group called themselves 'The Forget-me-nots Social Group'.

Having delivered the group for 18 months, an independent evaluation of the Forget-me-nots Group has been completed. The feedback from participants has highlighted that group members feel that:

- Holding group meetings in a family friendly environment allows those attending to reconnect with their families.

- The group provides an opportunity to form close friendships with respect to shared understandings of living with young onset dementia.

- The group brings people from different social contexts together such that the group helps to widen the social horizons of members.

- The group context provides a positive environment in which the normality of behaviours in the context of the condition are emphasised.

For the person with dementia, as well as their family and friends, to keep as well as possible following their diagnosis, it is important that all involved remain as socially connected as possible. It is therefore important for practitioners who work with them to spend time with them listening to their life stories, to identify who they are, what they like and dislike, and what activities they would choose to participate in. It is important that all members of the family are supported to keep in touch with friends and the wider community by continuing to be an active member of any community groups or organisations which are valuable and important to sustaining their social life outside the family home. It is also essential that both the person with dementia and family carers are supported to stay physically and mentally active, this may be via existing community-based support groups or by joining new groups, like the Forget-me-nots Group, which have been specifically designed for people with young onset dementia and their families. Practitioners should be able to 'signpost' to appropriate community-based social support groups if required.

A diagnosis of dementia does not mean that the person can no longer form new relationships. In fact, there may be comfort in being able to share with other people in similar circumstances to gain a sense of peer support and reduce the feelings of isolation. There can be strong mental and physical health benefits to continuing to expand the social circle of both the family and their loved one. Specialist social support groups are a very beneficial way of staying socially connected with people in similar circumstances in a safe space with specialist support. It is therefore vital that practitioners, adopting a person-centred approach, facilitate and support the continuance of such groups and support the person with dementia and their family to attend them should they wish to.

Conclusion

As this chapter has demonstrated, a key element of interventions promoting participation in social activities appears to be that they serve as a communication channel for people with dementia to engage, interact and talk with others, also referred to as collective engagement (Jones *et al.* 2015). Besides connecting people to others, participation in social activities can provide empowerment, information and education, pleasure and contribute to a reduction of cognitive deterioration (Kuiper *et al.* 2015). Active engagement and participation in meaningful activities and social interactions are essential for promoting social health and wellbeing for people living with the effects of dementia. For younger people with dementia, generic dementia support groups are often perceived as not appropriate for them as the differences between their needs and older people with dementia are considerable. As such, social support groups for people with young onset dementia and their families, which provide practical information, knowledge and education, as well as social support, can fill a gap in service provision. The fact that such groups are specifically designed for people living with young onset dementia is particularly pertinent as the value of sharing experiences with others in similar circumstances can help them come to terms with their changed lives.

KEY POINTS

1. A diagnosis of dementia can have a significant psychosocial impact on both the individual and their family in terms of reducing social connection, and increasing loneliness and isolation.

2. Specialist social support groups can be extremely beneficial in maintaining relationships both within the family and the wider community.

3. Health and social care practitioners should adopt a person-centred approach when signposting to appropriate specialist support and other appropriate community-based interventions.

References

Allen, J., Oyebode, J. R. and Allen J. (2009) 'Having a father with young onset dementia. The impact on well-being of young people.' *Dementia* 8, 455–480.

Baumeister, R.F., DeWall, C.N., Ciarocco, N.J. and Twenge, J.M. (2005) 'Social exclusion impairs self-regulation.' *Journal of Personality and Social Psychology 88*, 4, 589–604.

Baumeister, R.F. and Leary, M.R. (1995) 'The need to belong: Desire for interpersonal attachments as a fundamental human motivation.' *Psychological Bulletin 117*, 3, 497–529.

Beattie, A., Daker-White, G. and Means, R. (2004) '"How can they tell?" A qualitative study of the views of younger people about their dementia and dementia care services.' *Health and Social Care in Community 12*, 359–368.

Brooker, D. (2007) *Person-Centred Dementia Care: Making Services Better.* London: Jessica Kingsley Publishers.

Brooker, D.J., Argyle, E., Scally, A.J. and Clancy, D. (2011) 'The enriched opportunities programme for people with dementia: A cluster-randomised controlled trial in 10 extra care housing schemes.' *Aging and Mental Health 15*, 8, 1008–1017.

Cacioppo, J.T. and Patrick W. (2008) *Loneliness: Human Nature and the Need for Social Connection.* New York: W.W. Norton and Company.

Charras, K. (2011) 'Familiarity and domesticity: The Eval'zheimer (R) way of life.' *International Psychogeriatrics 23*, Suppl 1, S216–S217.

Clemerson, G., Walsh, S. and Isaac, C. (2014) 'Towards living well with young onset dementia: An exploration of coping from the perspective of those diagnosed.' *Dementia 13*, 4, 451–466.

Cohen-Mansfield, J., Dakheel-Ali, M. and Marx, M. S. (2009) 'Engagement in persons with dementia: the concept and its measurement.' *The American Journal of Geriatric Psychiatry 17*, 4, 299–307.

Cohen, S. and Wills, T.A. (1985) 'Stress, social support, and the buffering hypothesis.' *Psychological Bulletin 98*, 310–357.

de Bruin, S.R., Oosting, S.J., Kuin, Y., Hoefnagels, E.C., Blauw, Y.H., Groot, L.C.D. and Schols, J.M. (2009) 'Green care farms promote activity among elderly people with dementia.' *Journal of Housing for the Elderly 23*, 4, 368–389.

Dröes, R.M., Meiland, F., Schmitz, M. and van Tilburg, W. (2004) 'Effect of combined support for people with dementia and carers versus regular day care on behaviour and mood of persons with dementia: Results from a multi-centre implementation study.' *International Journal of Geriatric Psychiatry 19*, 7, 673–684.

Hawkins, S., McAiney, C., Denton, M. and Ploeg, J. (2013) 'The social experiences of spouses of persons with young-onset dementia (YOD): Social change, support and resiliency.' *Alzheimer's and Dementia 9*, 324.

Huber, M., Knottnerus, J.A., Green, L., van der Horst, H., Jadad, A.R., Kromhout, D. and Smid, H. (2011) 'How should we define health?' *British Medical Journal 343*, d4163.

Johannessen, A. and Moller, A. (2013) 'Experiences of persons with early-onset dementia: A qualitative study.' *Dementia 12*, 410–424.

Jones, C., Sung, B., and Moyle, W. (2015) 'Assessing engagement in people with dementia: A new approach to assessment using video analysis.' *Archives of Psychiatric Nursing 29*, 6, 377–382.

Kawachi, I. and Berkman, L.F., (2001) 'Social ties and mental health.' *Journal of Urban Health: Bulletin of the New York Academy of Medicine 78*, 3, 458–467.

Kitwood, T. (1997) *Dementia Reconsidered: The Person Comes First.* Buckingham: Open University Press.

Kok, B.E., Coffey, K.A., Cohn, M.A., Catalino, L.L. *et al.* (2013) 'How positive emotions build physical health: Perceived positive social connections account for the upward spiral between positive emotions and vagal tone.' *Psychological Science 24*, 7, 1123–1132.

Kuiper, J.S., Zuidersma, M., Oude Voshaar, R.C., Zuidema, S.U., van den Heuvel, E.R., Stolk, R.P. and Smidt, N. (2015) 'Social relationships and risk of dementia: A systematic review and meta-analysis of longitudinal cohort studies.' *Ageing Research Reviews 22*, 39–57.

Lockeridge, S. and Simpson, J. (2012) 'The experience of caring for a partner with young onset dementia: How younger carers cope.' *Dementia 0*, 0, 1–17.

Masi, C.M., Chen H., Hawkley, C.L. and Cacioppo J.T. (2011) 'A meta-analysis of interventions to reduce loneliness.' *Personality and Social Psychology Review 15*, 3, 219–266.

O'Rourke, H.M., Duggleby, W., Fraser, K.D. and Jerke, L. (2015) 'Factors that affect quality of life from the perspective of people with dementia: a metasynthesis.' *Journal of American Geriatric Society 63*, 1, 24–38.

Park, A.-L. (2014) 'Is there anything special about intergenerational approaches to older people with dementia? A review.' *Journal of Alzheimer's Disease and Parkinsonism 4*, 172.

Parkes, J.H. and Ward, A. (2015) 'The Forget-me-nots Social Group for People with Young Onset Dementia and their carers: Celebrating the group's success one year on.' *Journal of Dementia Care 23*, 4, 20–21.

Verbeek, H., Zwakhalen, S.M., van Rossum, E., Ambergen, T., Kempen, G.I. and Hamers, J.P. (2014) 'Effects of small-scale, home-like facilities in dementia care on residents' behavior, and use of physical restraints and psychotropic drugs: A quasi-experimental study.' *International Psychogeriatrics 26*, 4, 657–668.

CHAPTER 7

Meaningful Occupation and Activities

Rationale

Evidence suggests that most people of working age who receive a diagnosis of dementia choose to voluntarily leave work (Travis 2014). This may be because they feel the work or environment is too challenging and they feel no longer able to cope. The consequences of this decision can have psychological, social, and financial implications for both the individual and their family. However, with effective family, employer, and clinical support, having a diagnosis of dementia may not mean that either the person with the diagnosis or their family will have to cease employment.

The aim of this chapter is to consider the impact on the person of working age and their family of having a diagnosis of dementia. It will explore how employees can be supported by their employers and reasonable adjustments can be made in the workplace. Should the individual feel no longer able to cope in paid employment, the chapter highlights how practitioners can support them to make the decision to stop working, and explore alternative occupations which will provide a sense of purpose, value, and meaning.

Learning objectives

The learning objectives for this chapter are to:

- Explore how a person with dementia and/or their family can be supported in continued employment after receiving a diagnosis.

- Identify how employers can make reasonable adjustments to support their employee in continued employment.

- Consider how health and social care practitioners can support the individual and their family once they decide to stop working.

Introduction

For human beings, there is an innate desire to be actively engaged in meaningful occupations (Reilly 1962; Wilcock 1993; Yerxa 1998). The reasons why people choose to work vary from person to person. For most people, the principal motivation is financial reward. We go to work to earn money to pay the household bills, educate the children, save for our retirement, support our interests and hobbies, and finance our leisure pursuits, such as holidays (Hammell 2004). However, the desire and ability to work, whether it is paid, unpaid, or indeed voluntary, can have a significant effect on our physical and mental wellbeing (Clarke 2011; Wilcock 2011). A positive working environment can provide a sense of teamwork, togetherness, and camaraderie among co-workers. Individuals can get personal satisfaction from completing tasks, getting positive feedback, and feeling that they are making a contribution to the overall mission of the organisation. Some people just love to work to be busy, active, and achieve their own personal goals in life.

Working, paid or unpaid, can impact on an individual's morale, motivation, and overall quality of life (Christian and Townsend 2010). People also choose to work in order to feel confident, appreciated, valued, and of worth to society (Meyer 1922; 1977). The workplace can also be a source of 'social cohesion' (Warr 1996); people go to work to meet and interact with others and participate in social and community networks. Whatever the reasons people have for working, the fact that they choose to work can mean that they are engaged in work-related activities for a significant part of the week.

For younger people of working age, the gradual cognitive changes associated with a dementia, such as personality, behaviour, memory or reasoning can have a significant impact on their ability to undertake their role at work and complete their usual daily tasks. It may be possible to continue to work if reasonable and realistic workplace adjustments can be made. This will mean that in the early stages, the employer and the person with a diagnosis may need to make reasonable adjustments to support continued employment. Eventually, however, the person may feel that the nature of the work becomes too much for them, at this time, they should be supported by their employer and key worker to make the best decision for them and their family. Having made the decision to stop paid work, the key worker should actively encourage the individual to explore alternative meaningful occupations outside of the family home. Eventually, as dementia progresses, the employee will be faced with the decision of when to give up work. It is imperative at this point that they are empowered and supported to make that decision at a time that is appropriate for them, their family, and the employer.

The impact on the person of working age and their family of a diagnosis of dementia

Having a dementia at any age is traumatic for both the person with a diagnosis and their family; but for a person of working age, it can have 'devastating consequences for productivity, family and society' (Bakker *et al.* 2008; Fadil *et al.* 2009, van Vliet *et al.* 2012). The person with dementia can experience significant alterations to their sense of self, experience multiple losses (independence, social status, and roles) and develop feelings of dependency, loneliness, and social isolation as their mental abilities gradually decline (Pipon-Young *et al.* 2012). The impact of dementia can also have serious implications on the financial stability of their family. Typically, in young onset dementia, the person diagnosed is still working when they are first diagnosed, which means they could be the main family wage earner, or at least be providing a full or partial salary into the family home (Travis 2014). In addition, the spouse or partner can choose to adopt more flexible working practices, reduce their hours, take early retirement, or leave employment altogether so they can cope with their caring role. Either the person with dementia or the spouse/partner becoming unemployed can result in economic, social and emotional burdens being faced by their families. The impact is potentially a reduction in household income, less interaction with family, friends and the wider community, more time spent in each other's company and increasingly fewer opportunities for both the person with dementia and their family to actively engage in meaningful occupation outside of the family home (Harris and Keady 2004). However, receiving a diagnosis of dementia does not always mean that the person must stop working, at least in the first few years. As we already know, everybody with a dementia is unique. Therefore, it will very much depend on the nature of their symptoms and the effect on the job role they are undertaking as to whether realistic workplace adjustments can be made in order to support the ongoing employment of the person with a dementia.

As we already know, it is notoriously difficult to diagnose a dementia in a younger person in the early stages of the disease, as the initial signs can differ significantly from those observed in individuals with a later onset (van Vliet *et al.* 2012). For many people of working age, as described by Wendy and Anne below, they often state that they first noticed the early signs while still working (Chaplin and Davidson 2016; Evans 2016).

> I was notorious for having a brilliant memory but it began to let me down badly. I'd be in meetings and forget the simplest of words. I'd forget the names of people I'd been working with for years. The worst occasion happened at work, when I came out of my office one day; an office I'd been in for a couple of years; yet I didn't know where I was or who all the voices around me belonged to. It was then I accepted that things just weren't right. (Wendy)

Many people exhibiting the signs and symptoms associated with a young onset dementia have already left employment prior to being formally diagnosed. However, in the case of Anne, she was able, supported by her partner and employer, to take her own decision to leave employment after receiving her diagnosis (see Case study 7.1).

CASE STUDY 7.1

I was 55 in 2015, when I realised there was something wrong as I was making spelling mistakes and becoming hesitant as I spoke, especially at work. As an English graduate, a civil servant for 35 years and now a company secretary, I had always been very confident in writing and speaking. Having spoken to my GP, I was referred to two consultants for tests and, in August 2016, Dr xxx gave me my diagnosis of Primary Progressive Apraxia with Alzheimer's. Until this point, I had not told anybody at work about my problems, mainly because I didn't know what it they were myself. A core part of my role was to take the minutes of the Board and advise members on governance and decision-making. This was becoming increasingly difficult as my handwriting became worse and I was less confident in meetings. I worked from home more so that I could dictate documents and e-mails without anybody seeing the issues. As soon as we had the diagnosis, my partner and I decided that I would seek ill-health retirement and leave work as soon as possible so I may focus on looking after my health and wellbeing. I told my CEO and HR contact and both were very supportive and agreed that it was my decision whom I told and when. I told a small number of colleagues and their support was helpful over the next months as I knew there were people there that I could rely on. Because of my role, I did not tell other colleagues until I was sure I was leaving, as I was concerned that some may challenge my ability once they knew about my illness. That worked well for me and the College. By far the worst part of all the process was dealing with the external bodies who managed the occupational health and pension schemes. Even being a bureaucrat myself, and with the support of my partner, my company and one of the most eminent Professors in the country on this illness, it was 10 months before I was able to retire. It was hard to find the strength to deal with volume of papers and the repetition of the questions and answers and there were errors in their reports, such as suggesting that I was still able to drive work when I have never driven! I would advise anybody to start the process as soon possible and have support in dealing with the paperwork. A member of the Alzheimer's Society was in the room when I had my diagnosis and she has been a major support for me and my partner since. I would suggest that the information that the society can provide would be helpful to anybody in this situation.

According to Hunt (2011), Travis (2014) and Evans (2016) it is invariably co-workers who first notice that their colleague is behaving 'out of character for them' while engaged in familiar jobs and activities at work. They report seeing changes in mood, personality, and behaviour. They may not always attribute these changes to a decline in mental abilities, but they see their colleague forget appointments, unable to complete formerly well-known and understood tasks, witness an inability to plan and problem solve, a struggle with words and language, and difficulty in understanding the perspectives of other team members. At this point, it is critical that any person exhibiting a deviation from their normal behaviour is supported in seeking help and advice as to how to manage these apparent cognitive alterations, as there are potentially a number of reasons why someone might be experiencing an inability to perform their usual daily tasks at work. These might include physical ill health, medication changes, drug or alcohol use, excessive or prolonged stress, anxiety and depression.

Once the person has received a formal diagnosis, they will need to consider whether they wish to continue working or not. At this stage, it is important that the person with the diagnosis discusses this with their family, human resources department, occupational health or line manager and if necessary seek independent employment advice. The Alzheimer's Society also provides information which may also be helpful (see the Resources section at the end of the book). Additionally, they and their family should be supported by their appropriate health and social care team to make the decision that is right for all involved. As soon as a formal diagnosis has been made, the practitioners involved with the person with dementia and their family should ensure that they receive all the necessary information available to them about work-related and health benefits and entitlements in order to help and support them to make a fully informed decision. For example, the Young People with Dementia Service (YPDS) Cambridge and Peterborough NHS Foundation Trust work with people with dementia to inform them about what they may be entitled to (see Box 7.1).

Box 7.1: The Young People with Dementia Service Cambridgeshire & Peterborough NHS Foundation Trust

In North Cambridgeshire, the aim of the service for Young People with Dementia[1] is to enable them to remain as independent as possible in the community. They therefore work closely with the memory clinics to identify those who have recently received a diagnosis and their carers, and then visit them in their own homes to offer support, information and advice. This includes carrying out specialist assessments, developing complex care plans, commissioning care, undertaking ongoing reviews, signposting to other support agencies, and giving information alongside practical, psychological and emotional support. This can be about:

---

1   www.cpft.nhs.uk/help/young-onset-dementia_2.htm

- personal independence payments and employment support allowance applications

- care allowances

- state pension (where applicable)

- child tax credits (where children are involved).

They also provide help and support, including assisting with:

- debt recovery services

- HM Revenue and Customs

- employers

- the Independent Advocacy Service occupational and private pension providers

- legal issues, i.e. completing lasting power of attorney and court of protection applications on behalf of families.

The YPDS also advocates on behalf of people who may not have retired to try to ensure pensions are granted in full on medical grounds (Ramluggan and Ogo 2016).

Making the decision to continue to work following the diagnosis

Being able to maintain a person who has been recently diagnosed in work can be highly beneficial for both the individual themselves, as well as enriching the lives of all involved (Robertson and Evans 2015). Continuing in employment can help the person with dementia to feel that they still have a purpose in life. It can help them to feel good about themselves as they continue to contribute to the household finances, as well as feeling they still have value in society. Being able to work also helps them to continue to use their existing knowledge and skills, as well as possibly even learning new ones. This, in turn, enhances self-esteem and confidence as well as demonstrating to others that they have retained physical capabilities and mental capacities (Ebbitt, Burns and Christensen 1989). Finally, remaining in work for as long as possible encourages the continuance of workplace interactions and relationships, as well as sustaining on-going community and social networks. Ultimately, being able to go on working for as long as is practicable means that the person with dementia, as well as their spouse/partner, are able to remain socially connected and maintain a degree of financial stability during the early years following diagnosis.

For the person with dementia, with the support of their family, if they wish to carry on working, it is important that they speak to their employer as soon as they feel able to do so in order for reasonable, practical, and realistic adjustments can be made to the work environment to assist them to continue to do their job, albeit in a modified form. Under the Equality Act 2010, dementia is classed as a disability. This means that employers are required, where possible to make reasonable adjustments to ensure that individuals with a diagnosis are not disadvantaged or discriminated against in the workplace. It also affords employees with greater legal protection from being encouraged to take early retirement or face formal dismissal. Similarly, the Flexible Working Regulations (Sawyer 2006) require employers to consider the requests from carers for flexible working practices where these can be accommodated within the organisation.

Having disclosed their diagnosis to their employer, the person with dementia will then usually be asked to attend the organisation's Occupational Health Service where they should be offered specialist advice and support. At this stage, it is critical that the employee is honest and open about what they still can and cannot do, so that both parties can identify a range of possible solutions to any specific aspects of the role that are causing concerns. An action plan may be developed in partnership with the employee to identify what reasonable and realistic adjustments could be made by the organisation to assist them to be effective and feel supported at work. There are a number of ways that the person's workload and working practices can be adjusted to help them to cope better in the workplace (see Box 7.2).

Box 7.2: Reasonable adjustments employers could make in the workplace

- Looking at the current workload in terms of allocating tasks individually rather than all at once, and matching specific tasks with current abilities.

- Restructuring the way a person works. This might include simplifying the routines, providing quieter work spaces to reduce noise, interruptions, and distractions, and providing gaps and free time during the day to limit the effects of tiredness on cognitive functioning.

- Providing assistive technology and encouraging the use of memory aids to help the person with getting, storing, and recalling information. It is useful to help the person draw on their extensive previous learning experiences and knowledge to aid mental functioning.

- Identifying a colleague who can provide individual support to buddy up with the individual. It might also be beneficial to discuss the workplace adjustments with the wider team so they can understand why they are necessary, and also help to provide positive support.

- Providing positive visual and verbal encouragement to continue to work if required. It is not always the case that the person appears to be tired or disinterested, some people may respond well to verbal cues to begin or end a particular task or activity.

- Modifying their existing role. Reducing their responsibilities by delegating some duties to other team members.

- Having considered any financial implications first, it may be necessary for the employee to reduce their hours, take a lower grade, or even change roles and responsibilities within the organisation.[2]

Being able to carry on as long as possible at work may help the person with dementia and their family cope with the diagnosis as they will be able to retain some confidence in their existing knowledge and skills, stay connected through the company of work colleagues, and maintain a

---

2   Adapted from http://www.alzwisc.org/employerguides/EmployerGuide.pdf;
     http://theconversation.com/employers-must-become-aware-of-dementia-in-
     the-workplace-28125

clearly defined daily routine. However, for those individuals who are self-employed, there will also be contractual obligations to consider; for example, it may be up to them what personal adjustments they make in order to continue to actively contribute within their own business, but they should also consider the impact of their diagnosis on any business partners or company employees. Due to safety implications, some occupations also legally require the person with dementia to inform them of their condition, for example the armed forces or where dangerous machinery is being operated. There may also be a requirement to inform professional bodies about a diagnosis as it could affect professional status. In May 2017, the Royal College of Nursing suggested that the NHS should be a role model when it comes to employing nurses who have been diagnosed with dementia:

> Nurses who are diagnosed with dementia should keep their jobs and be allowed to continue caring for patients, the profession's trade union has demanded. The Royal College of Nursing said the health service should 'set an example' to the rest of society by allowing staff with the degenerative condition to carry on working. The organisation insisted nurses with the disease could continue practising without posing a risk to patients, but safety groups branded the proposal 'frightening and extraordinary'. (*The Telegraph* 2017)

Making the decision to stop working: Implications for practice

For most people, having a sense of meaning and purpose in life is vitally important, and this is no different for people diagnosed with a dementia. For younger people who have just stopped working, they could feel that they now have a lot of time on their hands without something meaningful to do in their everyday lives. According to Sperlinger and Furst (1994) and Travis (2014), most people of working age who receive a diagnosis of dementia decide to discontinue employment voluntarily. This is because they have found that, even with a supportive employer, the nature of the work has perhaps become too challenging and overwhelming. This may leave them feeling that they have 'failed' to cope, and are gradually in danger of losing their self-confidence, skills, dignity, independence, and social connections. In order to counteract some of these perceptions and associated feelings, it is important that the services, organisations, and key workers working with the individual and their family encourage them to continue to actively engage in meaningful activities which are interesting and important to them and which will support their autonomy and independence, preserve their dignity, enhance self-confidence and esteem, and help to maintain better psychological wellbeing and health-related quality of life.

Services involved with the person and their family should work with them to explore alternative sources of meaningful occupations outside of the family home, which could help to alleviate some of the negative consequences of giving up work. These might include part-time employment, volunteering, further study, participating in community social groups and activities, and engaging in campaigning and fundraising activities. YoungDementia UK present a case study of Keith, who was diagnosed with young onset Alzheimer's disease at 55; he describes how he volunteers as a dementia envoy:

I promote awareness of young onset dementia and support other people who share a similar diagnosis.

One door does open as one closes and my life, like that of many others, has been filled with different activities, rewards and interests since retiring – in fact life couldn't be busier and more varied! (YoungDementia UK 2017)

Wendy also describes how since she received her diagnosis, she has got involved in campaigning activities, such as public speaking and getting actively involved in research (see Case study 7.2).

CASE STUDY 7.2

We all had talents before a diagnosis of dementia entered our world, we don't suddenly lose all those talents overnight when given that diagnosis. Many people seem to forget this. Sadly, the postcode lottery of available support meant services were sadly lacking. After the initial isolation and feelings of abandonment, I found the strength and personal resilience to adapt to a new way of living, to help myself instead of going into a state of depression. Strangely enough, dementia has opened up for me new opportunities. Many of these I now call the 'advantages of living with dementia'. It's so important to see the positives in order to cope with the daily struggles that dementia throws at you each day. I use to be a very private person but was so shocked at the lack of awareness and understanding of dementia, not only from the public, but healthcare professionals as well, that I'm now willing to shout from the rooftops about the reality of living with dementia. Public speaking has allowed me to reach people I would not necessarily meet in everyday life. My newfound passion for research has enabled me to work with many researchers. Writing my blog has enabled me, not only to have a constant reminder of the things I've achieved, but to reach others around the world and raise awareness. All this, I call, 'my Sudoku' as it enables me to expose my failing brain to many new conversations and activities, all of which provides valuable stimulation and feelings of being valued.

In order to effectively support the individual to create new activities or access existing suitable community-based activities which are appropriate to their strengths, limitations, and interests, and which are purposeful to them, it is essential that key people involved with them spend time in getting to know the person behind the dementia in terms of their lived experiences, existing knowledge and skills, retained mental capacities and capabilities, likes and dislikes, hobbies and interests, and motivational levels. It is essential that the person with dementia should stipulate what activities they find meaningful and enjoyable and those they would not choose to participate in. Some leisure pursuits can fulfil the criteria of having a meaning, purpose or function, having value, and being important to the individual.

Engagement in these activities can generate feelings of enjoyment, pleasure, and happiness. They can lift mood and improve energy levels. Having positive experiences to plan and look forward to can encourage the individual to continue to take care of their personal appearance. Finally, having a sense of purpose, productivity, ongoing value, and clear routines can provide the person with dementia with a clear balance between rest and restorative activity that continues to exercise and challenge the brain. This in turn clearly demonstrates to themselves, their family, and wider society that they are still a person with preferences, hopes, dreams, and aspirations (Chaplin 2003).

Conclusions

The need to be actively engaged in occupations which are meaningful does not change for someone living with dementia, particularly in the case of those who are of working age. These individuals still need to feel valuable, productive, and have a purpose in life. It is therefore essential that practitioners who are working with people with a young onset dementia listen to what is of interest and importance to that individual. In this way they can effectively support them to find alternative sources of occupations that will help to compensate for the loss of paid employment. Such activities may come in the form of unpaid work, fundraising and campaigning opportunities, and new leisure pursuits, hobbies, and interests.

KEY POINTS

1. The person with a diagnosis and their family should be at the heart of all decisions made about the desire to continue or stop working.

2. Employers should be supported by health and social care practitioners to make realistic and reasonable adjustments for their employees with a diagnosis.

3. Once the person with dementia has made the decision to stop paid work, their health and social care team should assist them to explore alternative sources of occupations.

4. The benefits of continuing to engage in meaningful activities include having a purpose in life, feeling productive and of value, retaining existing knowledge and skills, and maintaining self-confidence in own abilities and ongoing mental capacities.

References

Bakker, C., De Vugt, M.E., van Vliet, D., Verhey, F.R.J., Pijnenburg, Y.A., Vernooij-Dassen, M. and Koopmans, R.T.C (2008) 'The use of formal and informal care in early onset dementia: Results from the NeedYD study.' *The American Journal of Geriatric Psychiatry 21*, 1, 37–45.

Chaplin, R. (2003) 'Occupational Therapy Interventions.' In R. Baldwin and M. Murray (eds) *Younger People with Dementia*. New York, NY: Martin Dunitz.

Chaplin, R. and Davidson, I. (2016) 'What are the experiences of people with dementia in employment?' *Dementia 15*, 2, 147–161.

Christiansen, C.H. and Townsend, E.A. (eds) (2010) *Introduction to Occupation: The Art and Science of Living (2nd edition)*. Upper Saddle River, NJ: Prentice Hall.

Clark, F. (2011) 'Reflections on the human as an occupational being: Biological need, tempo and temporality.' *Journal of Occupational Science 4*, 3, 86–92.

Ebbitt, B., Burns, T. and Christensen, R. (1989) 'Work therapy: Intervention for community-based Alzheimer's patients.' *American Journal of Alzheimer's Disease and Other Dementias 4*, 5, 7–15.

Evans, D. (2016) 'An exploration of the impact of younger-onset dementia on employment.' Accessed on 17/10/17 at http://journals.sagepub.com/doi/pdf/10.1177/1471301216668661

Fadil, H., Borazanci, A., Ait Ben Haddou, E., Yahyaoui, M., Korniychuk, E., Jaffe, S.L. and Minagar, A. (2009) 'Chapter 13 Early Onset Dementia.' *International Review of Neurobiology 84*, 245–262.

Hammell, K.W. (2004) 'Dimensions of meaning in the occupations of daily life.' *Canadian Journal of Occupational Therapy 71*, 5, 296–305.

Harris, P. and Keady, J. (2004) 'Living with early onset dementia: Exploring the experience and developing evidence-based guidelines for practice.' *Alzheimer's Care Quarterly 5*, 2, 111–122.

Hunt, C. D. (2011). 'Young-onset dementia: A review of the literature and what it means for clinicians.' *Journal of Psychosocial Nursing 49*, 29–33.

Meyer, A. (1977) 'The philosophy of occupation therapy.' *American Journal of Occupational Therapy 31*, 639–642.

Ministers of the Crown (2010) *Equality Act 2010*. London: The Stationery Office Limited.

Pipon-Young, F.E., Lee, K.M., Jones, F. and Guss, R. (2012) 'I'm not all gone, I can still speak: The experiences of younger people with dementia. An action research study.' *Dementia 11*, 5, 597–616.

Ramluggan, P. and Ogo, E., (2016) 'Young onset dementia service provision and its effect on service users and family members.' *Mental Health Practice 19*, 10, 15–19.

Reilly, M. (1962) 'Occupational therapy can be one of the great ideas of 20th century medicine, 1961 Eleanor Clarke Slagle lecture.' *American Journal of Occupational Therapy 16*, 1–9.

Robertson, J. and Evans, D. (2015) 'Evaluation of a workplace engagement project for people with younger onset dementia.' *Journal of Clinical Nursing 24*, 15–16, 2331–2339.

Sperlinger, D. and Furst, M. (1994) 'The service experiences of people with presenile dementia: A study of carers in one London borough.' *International Journal of Geriatric Psychiatry 9*, 47–50.

Sawyer, H. (2006) *The 2006 United Kingdom Flexible Working Act.* Produced on behalf of Workplace Flexibility 2010 by the Georgetown Federal Legislation Clinic. Georgetown: Georgetown University Law Center.

Travis, C. (2014) *Experiencing dementia in the workplace: impacts of younger onset dementia on employment.* Master's and Doctoral Projects. 603. Accessed on 17/10/17 at http://utdr.utoledo.edu/graduate-projects/603

Telegraph, The (2017) 'Nurses with dementia should be allowed to keep their jobs, says Royal College of Nursing' 15 May. Accessed on 17/10/17 at www.telegraph.co.uk/news/2017/05/15/nurses-dementia-should-allowed-keep-jobs-says-royal-college

Van Vliet, D., de Vugt, M.E., Kohler, S., Aalten, P. *et al.* (2012) 'Awareness and its association with affective symptoms in young-onset and late-onset Alzheimer disease: A prospective study.'*Alzheimers Disease & Associated Disorders 27*, 3, 265–271.

Warr, P. (1996) *Psychology at Work (4th edition)* London: Penguin Books.

Wilcock, A. (1993) 'A theory of the human need for occupation.' *Journal of Occupational Science 1*, 1, 17–24.

Wilcock, A.A. (2011) 'Occupation and health: Are they one and the same?' *Journal of Occupational Science 14*, 1, 3–8.

Yerxa, E. (1998) 'Health and the human spirit for occupation.' *American Journal of Occupational Therapy 52*, 412–418.

YoungDementia UK (2017) *Volunteering.* Oxford: YDUK. Accessed 11/09/17 at www.youngdementiauk.org/volunteering

Conclusions

The care and support of people with young onset dementia presents as an interesting challenge for health and social care practitioners, appropriate services and organisations, and indeed policy makers. There are complexities in the diagnosis and subsequent treatment, and there is a lack of age appropriate service provision for the needs of this younger age group. However, by producing this book, the authors are providing those formal and informal carers and families who care and support them on a daily basis with enhanced knowledge and understanding of the physical, social and psychological impact of the diagnosis for all involved in the dementia care journey. The hope is that a more family-focused approach, which promotes positive post diagnostic support, can assist the person with dementia to remain as independent as possible at home, supported by their family and wider social network.

Younger people with a diagnosis of dementia and their families have become increasingly more visible in the national campaign to challenge society's attitude to dementia. This has been galvanised further by the creation and formal launch of the Young Dementia Network in 2016, which aims to encourage improved services for younger people across the UK, by influencing policy makers, encouraging research and development into young onset dementia, creating and contributing to useful resources, and encouraging improved understanding among health and social care professionals. Yet despite the increased visibility of this group, receiving a timely and accurate diagnosis and gaining access to age-appropriate support continues to be challenging because dementia services remain primarily focused upon the needs of older people. Currently, there is limited evidence regarding the optimum clinical approach required for timely and accurate diagnosis, despite existing evidence recommending that improvements should be made. Equally, the essential elements of service provision for young people with dementia, including clear pathways into care, increased availability of more meaningful occupational and social activity; age-appropriate respite and long-term care are well established; however, there still appears to be limited or no provision of age-appropriate post diagnostic, respite and long-term support in most UK regions. To try to address this issue, University College London, the University of Bradford, the University of Northampton and the University of Surrey are conducting the Angela Project, a three-year project funded by the Alzheimer's Society, which seeks to improve diagnosis and post diagnostic support for younger people living with dementia and their caregivers across the UK. The hope is that the outcomes of this national study will inform policy makers and practitioners about the care pathways required for people with young onset dementia and their families.

Until the study findings are published in 2020, it is unlikely that care pathways will be formally established at a national level. However, in the meantime, more can be done by individual practitioners, services and organisations to support the person with dementia and their family at a local level, by understanding their experiences and circumstances, and signposting towards community-based and specialist support where available. This book also contributes to available resources and sources of information by providing practical guidelines to practitioners to help the family and individual live as positively as possible with a diagnosis.

The first key message to emerge from the pages of this book is the need for practitioners to appreciate the complexities surrounding the diagnosis of young onset dementia and its different types of presentation. In a person under the age of 65 years dementia may not be an initial consideration when they present with signs that could be mistaken for depression, anxiety, changes in mood or behaviour, particularly if loss of memory is not a symptom. However, a greater awareness of young onset dementia could reduce time to diagnosis and provide quicker referrals to specialist dementia services. An awareness of those who may be at an increased risk of developing dementia at a younger age could also assist with diagnosis. Those who have a family history of young onset dementia, and those with a learning disability – particularly Down syndrome – could be at an increased risk. A diagnosis can be further complicated by the person showing symptoms, who may not want to receive a diagnosis or may be in denial about the changes to their health; furthermore, they may not be aware of any changes – depending on their type of dementia. Talking with family members as part of the diagnostic process could identify issues which their symptomatic family member is not able to talk about. A person who has behavioural changes, becoming more aggressive or disinhibited, may not see their behaviour as having changed but rather believe that those around them have changed, in a case such as this, additional input into the diagnostic process becomes more essential.

The second key message presented to the reader is that, following the diagnosis, the person with dementia and families should be provided with appropriate advice regarding what help and support they can receive. While the impact on the family of a diagnosis can be considerable, there are ways to offer practical and psychological support. Working across professions and with the families to understand their needs is the starting point here. Whether it is providing counselling, occupational therapy, signposting to legal services or mentors for children, post diagnostic support for families living with the effects of young onset dementia can help them to understand what the diagnosis means and to make the necessary adjustments to deal with any issues which may arise.

Finally, the third key message that is offered to the reader, is that a diagnosis of dementia, while potentially devastating for all involved, does not necessarily mean that the person cannot live positively, with purpose, and independently for as long as possible, given the right information and support from those who care and support them.

A diagnosis of dementia can result in feelings of grief, guilt and depression, and the loss of relationships and friendships. Working with individuals and families to reconnect socially and to engage in social activities where they can meet other people and be part of normal social interactions is a positive way of offering support. Being with people who are going through a similar experience is particularly important for the person with the diagnosis and the family, as this brings with it understanding, learning and kinship. The impact on wellbeing can be positive, bringing feelings of empowerment, pleasure, improved communication, and for the person with dementia potentially a reduction in the degree of cognitive decline. In addition to supporting the social and leisure activities of families, supporting or encouraging meaningful occupations can increase a person's sense of purpose and value. Meaningful occupation could include helping a person remain at work, through adaptations or revised roles, taking on volunteering or even supporting people to take up campaigning on dementia. A number of key spokespeople for dementia, and those who have developed young onset dementia, have become advocates for raising awareness, promoting a 'nothing about us, without us' approach to service provision and care, through groups such as the Dementia Alliance International and the Dementia Engagement and Empowerment Project (see the Resources section). A diagnosis of dementia does not mean an end to what a person can contribute to wider society, to their community, friends or family. Neither does it mean that a person no longer has aspirations for their life or has preferences for how they are cared for. Finding ways to facilitate these preferences and aspirations is an important part of working with the individual and family to ensure these needs are met.

The stigma around dementia is reducing with campaigns such as the Alzheimer's Society Dementia Friends initiative, which seeks to raise awareness and reduce the fear a diagnosis can bring. Alongside such initiatives, the raised profile of dementia at a strategic and policy level during David Cameron's premiership has helped to bring dementia to the fore and contributed towards raising the knowledge and understanding of dementia. However, there is still more work to be done with raising awareness of young onset dementia, which remains a lesser known condition amongst the general population and health and social care professionals. We need to work towards raising awareness of young onset dementia and in developing the specialist services or groups which work to meet the needs of this age group.

What has been presented through the chapters in this book is the need for a greater understanding from health and social care professionals, services and organisations, and indeed policy makers of what young onset dementia means to those with the diagnosis and their families, and how they can best be supported to cope and adapt to the changes they will need to make to their lifestyles to be able to live as positively and independently for as long as is possible in the community.

Resources

Activity and support groups

The Dementia Engagement and Empowerment Project (DEEP): www.dementiavoices.org.uk

Dementia Adventures: www.dementiaadventure.co.uk

Young Dementia UK (Young Dementia Network): www.youngdementiauk.org

YPWD Berkshire West: www.ypwd.info/about-us

Charities

Age UK: www.ageuk.org.uk

Alzheimer's Research: www.alzheimersresearchuk.org

Alzheimer's Society: www.alzheimers.org.uk

British Institute of Learning Disability: www.bild.org.uk

Carers Trust: www.carers.org

Carers UK: www.carersuk.org

Citizens Advice: www.citizensadvice.org.uk

Dementia UK: www.dementiauk.org

Down's Syndrome Association: www.downs-syndrome.org.
uk

Foundation for People with Learning Disabilities:
www.mentalhealth.org.uk/learning-disabilities

Lewy Body Society: www.lewybody.org

Mencap: www.mencap.org.uk

Parkinson's UK: www.parkinsons.org.uk

Rare Dementias Support: www.raredementiasupport.org

Samaritans: www.samaritans.org

YoungDementia UK: www.youngdementiauk.org

Driving and accessible parking

To download a form to tell the DVLA about a dementia
diagnosis: www.gov.uk/dementia-and-driving

To apply for a blue badge online: www.gov.uk/apply-blue-
badge (England); www.mygov.scot (Scotland); www.gov.
wales/topics/transport/road-users/bluebadgeschemeinfo
(Wales); www.nidirect.gov.uk/information-and-services/
motoring-and-transport/blue-badgescheme (Northern
Ireland)

Education

Dementia Pathfinders: www.dementiapathfinders.org

Health Education England Tier 1 Dementia Awareness
training: www.hee.nhs.uk/our-work/person-centred-care/
dementia/tier-1-training

Social Care Institute for Excellence: www.scie.org.uk/
dementia/symptoms/young-onset

Wicking Dementia Research and Education Centre
University of Tasmania: Understanding Dementia MOOC:
www.utas.edu.au/wicking/understanding-dementia

Preventing Dementia MOOC: mooc.utas.edu.au/courses/
preventing-dementia-2017-03

Equipment and assistive technologies

AT Dementia is a charity that provides information and
advice on assistive technology for people with dementia.
Call 01157 484220. Visit www.atdementia.org.uk

Living made easy is an impartial advice and information
website about daily living equipment and other aspects of
independent living. It has been developed by the Disabled
Living Foundation. Call the helpline on 0300 999 0004
from 10am–4pm, Tuesday, Wednesday and Thursday. Visit
www.livingmadeeasy.org.uk

Unforgettable.org is a website that offers specialised
products for people living with dementia. Items range from
health and wellbeing products and gifts to mobility and
hygiene. It also offers advice and an online community.
Contact Unforgettable on 0203 322 9070 from 8am–8pm,
seven days a week. Visit www.unforgettable.org

Financial support

Use the online Benefits Calculator to see the benefits you,
or the person you care for, might be entitled to: www.gov.
uk/benefits-calculators

Carers Allowance online: www.gov.uk/carers-allowance

Carer's Credit claim form online: www.gov.uk/carers-credit

Council Tax reduction: www.gov.uk/apply-council-tax-reduction

Disability premium: www.gov.uk/disability-premiums-income-support

Employment and Support Allowance: www.gov.uk/employment-support-allowance

Personal Independence Payment: www.gov.uk/pip

Personal Health Budget: Talk to your local NHS team who help you most often with your care.

Personal Budget: You can request information about a personal budget by contacting your social services department and asking for a Needs Assessment.

Health promotion

NHS Choices, The Eatwell Guide: www.nhs.uk/Livewell/Goodfood/Pages/the-eatwell-guide.aspx

NHS Choices, Health Tools: www.nhs.uk/Tools/Pages/Toolslibrary.aspx

Public Health England, One You: www.nhs.uk/oneyou

Helplines (dementia)

Admiral Nurse Dementia Helpline: 0800 888 6678 or email: helpline@dementiauk.org

Alzheimer Scotland: Dementia Helpline 0808 808 3000 or email: helpline@alzscot.org

Alzheimer's Society: National Dementia Helpline: 0300 222 1122

Alzheimer's Society Northern Ireland: 0300 222 1122

Wales Dementia Helpline: 0808 808 2235

Legal issues

Deputyship under the Court of Protection: www.gov.uk/become-deputy

Lasting Power of Attorney: www.gov.uk/power-of-attorney

Employment

Alzheimer's Society: www.alzheimers.org.uk/download/downloads/id/1016/living_with_dementia_-_employment.pdf

YoungDementia UK: www.youngdementiauk.org/working-advice-employers

Subject Index

Author Index